Peter Debray
Thomas Lehnen
Peter W. Oldham

Besser in

Englisch

10. Klasse

Realschule

Cornelsen
SCRIPTOR

Über die Autoren:
Peter Debray unterrichtet Englisch an einer Gesamtschule. Thomas Lehnen unterrichtet Englisch an einem Gymnasium. Peter Oldham ist Brite und erfahrener Redakteur und Autor von Lehrwerken für das Fach Englisch.

Bildquellen:
Bibliographisches Institut, Mannheim S. 54; A. Gomille, Frankfurt am Main S. 73; Dr. R. König, Preetz S. 73; MEV Verlag, Augsburg S. 105; picture-alliance/dpa, Frankfurt am Main S. 73, S. 80, S. 85, S. 87; picture-alliance/maxppp, Frankfurt am Main S. 27; shutterstock.com/Steve Adamson S. 73; shutterstock.com/CreativeHQ S. 73; shutterstock.com/fstockfoto S. 73; shutterstock.com/Jeanne Hatch S. 73; shutterstock.com/Patricia Hofmeester S. 73; shutterstock.com/Gregor Kervina S. 96; shutterstock.com/Sari O'Neal S. 73; shutterstock.com/Lincoln Rogers S. 73; ullstein bild/Imagebroker.net S. 65

Textquellen:
S. 66: Beini Shi: Not Asian Enough, www.layouth.com, Nov. – Dec. 2004 Issue; S. 70: Bob Herbert: "Failing Teachers", The New York Times, October 24, 2003; S. 79: Sam B.: Can I help you?, www.teenink.com; S. 86: Morton Rhue (Todd Strasser): The Wave, © 1981 by Dell Publishing, Inc. and T. A. T. Communications Company. Used by permission of Dell Publishing, a division of Random House, Inc., zitiert nach: Hamburg 1987, S. 86 f.; S. 93: Misha H.: Hidden Blue, www.teenink.com; S. 95: Polly Curtis: "Schools warned of pupils hooked on energy drinks", The Guardian, September 3, 2008; S. 109: Michael Hann: "Why we should step in to halt bad behaviour", The Guardian, September 3, 2008

Bibliografische Information der Deutschen Nationalbibliothek
Die Deutsche Nationalbibliothek verzeichnet diese Publikation in der Deutschen Nationalbibliografie; detaillierte bibliografische Daten sind im Internet über http://dnb.d-nb.de abrufbar.

2. Auflage

D C B A
Bibliographisches Institut GmbH, Dudenstraße 6, 68167 Mannheim

Redaktionelle Leitung: Constanze Schöder
Redaktion: lüra – Klemt & Mues GbR
Illustrationen: Bianca Schaalburg
Herstellung: Annette Scheerer
Layoutkonzept: Horst Bachmann, Weinheim
Umschlaggestaltung: glas AG, Seeheim-Jugenheim
Satz/Layout: Carola Fuchs, Berlin
Druck und Bindung: orthdruk, Białystok
Printed in Poland
ISBN 978-3-411-87084-4

Inhaltsverzeichnis

Liebe Schülerin, lieber Schüler,

du hast hier ein Buch zum Lernen, Wiederholen und Üben in der Hand.

- ▷ Die Themen sind in kleinen, verständlichen Schritten aufbereitet.
- ▷ Schaffe dir parallel zu diesem Buch ein Arbeitsheft an, in das du hineinschreiben kannst.
- ▷ Ein Lösungsheft hilft dir, deine Ergebnisse zu kontrollieren.
- ▷ Mit der beiliegenden CD und vielen Übungen dazu kannst du dein Hörverstehen trainieren. Folgender Hinweis zeigt dir, wo du die CD verwenden musst: **Track**

Mit diesem Buch kannst du auf zweierlei Weise arbeiten:

1. Möglichkeit:
Wenn du dich im Fach Englisch insgesamt ein wenig unsicher fühlst, solltest du das Buch von vorn bis hinten durcharbeiten. Nimm dir aber nicht zu viel auf einmal vor. Bearbeite lieber kleinere Abschnitte und arbeite dafür regelmäßig, vielleicht sogar täglich.

2. Möglichkeit:
Vielleicht kommst du eigentlich gut zurecht, hast aber einige Lücken? Kläre genau, am besten mithilfe deiner Lehrerin oder deines Lehrers, wo deine Lücken sind. Sieh im Inhaltsverzeichnis nach, wähle einzelne Abschnitte aus und arbeite sie durch.

GOOD TO KNOW | **Zum Arbeiten mit diesem Buch**

- ▶ Viele Aufgaben kannst du im Buch lösen. Benutze ein **Arbeitsheft,** wenn du viel schreiben musst.
- ▶ Bist du beim Lösen der Übungsaufgaben unsicher, schau dir die **Beispiele** dazu noch einmal an.
- ▶ Vergleiche deine Ergebnisse immer sorgsam mit dem **Lösungsheft**. Überprüfe genau, was du falsch gemacht hast. Aus Fehlern kann man gut lernen.
- ▶ Bearbeite dieselben Aufgaben nach einigen Tagen noch einmal. Die **Wiederholung** schafft Sicherheit.

Viel Spaß und Erfolg beim Lernen!

1 Revision: Sprache verstehen

Das solltest du am Ende der Klasse 10 können:

Alle grammatischen Strukturen verstehen und anwenden:
- ▷ Passiv
- ▷ *if*-Sätze
- ▷ Hilfsverben
- ▷ Alle Zeiten
- ▷ Indirekte Rede
- ▷ Infinitiv- und Gerundiumkonstruktionen
- ▷ Partizipien
- ▷ Artikel
- ▷ Konjunktionen
- ▷ Präpositionen

1.1 *The passive*

REMEMBER

Ein Aktivsatz betont die Person, die eine Handlung durchführt. Ein Passivsatz stellt dagegen die Person in den Hintergrund und betont die Handlung an sich.
Die Passivform des ***simple present*** wird mit am/is/are + Partizip Perfekt *(past participle)* gebildet.

Beispiele:

Aktivsatz:	Passivsatz:
Do people respect me?	Am I respected?
His wife tells him what to wear.	He is told what to wear (by his wife).

1 Read the interview and insert the following verbs in the simple present passive.

ask *attack* *break into* *call* *collect* *examine* *help*
justify *make* *report* *train* *treat*

1. A: Why ______ your book ______ „The Lonely Victim“?
2. B: Because when the central character‘s house ______ and he ______, he ______ not ______ by either the police or the justice system.
3. A: ______ this very negative opinion really ______?
4. B: Yes. In my experience, most police officers ______ not ______ ______ to deal with the victims of violent crimes.

5. A: What exactly happens when an attack ______ to the police?
6. B: Well, the victim ______ by a nurse or a doctor and physical evidence ______ .
7. A: And ______ these people ______ with respect?
8. B: Yes, but it's an unpleasant procedure and it ______ worse by the police. The victims ______ unnecessary and humiliating questions about their lifestyle.

REMEMBER *Present progressive passive*

Die Passivform des present progressive wird mit am/is/are + being + Partizip Perfekt gebildet.

Beispiele:

Aktivsatz:	Passivsatz:
Someone is calling my name.	My name **is being called.**
People are asking questions.	Questions **are being asked.**
We are planning a trip to New York.	A trip to New York **is being planned.**

2 Rewrite the active sentences as passive sentences.
Decide whether the subject of the active sentence is needed in the passive sentence.

1. Your cat is frightening my parrot.
2. People are treating him with contempt.
3. My computer is now updating its software.
4. The police are questioning two men about the incident.
5. Somebody is stealing money from the lockers in the changing room.
6. Those two girls over there are making fun of me!
7. Several workmen are erecting a stage for the open-air concert.

REMEMBER *Passive forms with modal verbs*

Aus einem Aktivsatz mit einem modalen Hilfsverb können zwei Passivformen gebildet werden. Die zweite Variante ist recht formell
und wird oft für offizielle Mitteilungen benutzt.

Beispiele:

Aktivsatz:	Passivsatz:
You must keep your dog on a leash.	(1) Dogs **must be kept** on a leash.
	(2) Dogs **are to be kept** on a leash.
The Queen will open the stadium.	(1) The stadium **will be opened** by ...
	(2) The stadium **is to be opened** by ...

3 Change the active sentences into both forms of the passive.

1. Passengers must show their boarding cards at the gate.
2. A flight attendant will explain the emergency landing drill.
3. Hotel guests should place their valuables in the hotel safe.
4. All visitors must display a visitor's pass.
5. Members must pay their annual fees by December 31.
6. Students can find a model answer at the end of the unit.
7. You shouldn't take her stories too seriously.
8. The general manager will present the annual report at the meeting.

REMEMBER *Impersonal passive*

Mit den folgenden passiven Wendungen drückt man aus, was allgemein angenommen wird:

be said to be believed to be thought to be supposed to be considered to

Beispiele:

He is said to be an excellent swimmer.	Er soll sehr gut schwimmen können.
He is believed to be staying in Egypt.	Es wird angenommen, dass er zu Besuch in Ägypten ist.
She was considered (to be) the best pianist of her generation.	Sie wurde für die beste Pianistin ihrer Generation gehalten.

4 Translate the following sentences into German.

1. Einstein and Da Vinci are considered to be geniuses.
2. He is said to be a very strange person.
3. She is thought to be lazy und unreliable.
4. His parents are generally believed to be extremely wealthy.
5. You are supposed to be charming, good-looking and very witty.

5 Fill in the missing information in this overview of passive forms.

Tense	Passive form		
1. simple present	am/is/are	+	past participle
2. present progressive	am/is/are being	+	past participle
3. simple past		+	past participle
4. past progressive		+	past participle
5. present perfect	has/have been	+	
6. past perfect		+	
7. will-future		+	
8. going to-future		+	

REMEMBER *Passive of verbs with two objects*

Manche Verben können im Aktivsatz mit zwei Objekten verbunden werden.
Beispiel:
Oxfam supplied the refugees with tents.
Das Personenobjekt (indirektes Objekt) ist refugees. Das Sachobjekt (direktes Objekt) ist tents. Folglich sind zwei Passivformen möglich:

1. Ein persönliches Passiv *(personal passive):*
   The refugees were supplied with tents.
2. Ein unpersönliches Passiv *(impersonal passive)*. Beachte das Anhängen von to vor dem Personenobjekt:
   Tents were supplied to the refugees.

Die folgenden Verben können zwei Objekten haben:
give offer tell promise send show supply

6 **Change the active sentences into both forms of the passive.**

1. A rival firm has offered me a better job.
2. The boss's secretary served us coffee and biscuits.
3. The mayor gave my mother an award for her work with a local charity.
4. The police showed us photos of criminals.
5. I sent an e-mail with some photos to my grandparents in Minsk.
6. My sister offered me a lift into town.
7. Mrs Brown gave all her pupils a small prize.
8. Dad showed our guests a video film of our last holiday.
9. We sent flowers to our grandmother.

1.2 *Conditional sentences*

REMEMBER *Conditional type I*

Bedingungssätze bestehen aus einem if-Nebensatz *(conditional clause)* mit einer Bedingung und einem Hauptsatz *(main clause)* mit einer Folge. Es gibt drei Arten von Bedingungssätzen: Typ I, II und III. Der if-Nebensatz kann vor oder nach dem Hauptsatz stehen. Steht der Hauptsatz zuerst, müssen die beiden Satzteile nicht mit einem Komma getrennt werden.

Conditional type I
Der Sprecher hält die Bedingung für real erfüllbar ***(real situation)***

Beispiele (mit Komma):	Beispiele (ohne Komma):
If I **go**, you **must go** with me.	You **must go** with me if I **go**.
If you **drop** it, it **will break**.	It **will break** if you **drop** it.

Das Verb im if-Nebensatz steht im *simple present*. Im Hauptsatz wird will/can/must + *infinitive* benutzt.

1 Choose the correct main clause for each conditional clause.

1. If we want to arrive on time,	A. you'll get fat.
2. If Liz brings her CD-player,	B. we can have a barbecue.
3. If you eat too much,	C. I won't take your photo.
4. If the weather is bad,	D. we must leave now.
5. If the weather is good,	E. he'll be in the semi-finals.
6. If you don't smile,	F. will you pay me £2?
7. If I wash and polish the car,	G. I'll bring my new CDs.
8. If Bob wins this game,	H. we'll stay at home and watch a film.

2 Rewrite the sentences above. Start with the main clause.

EXAMPLE

A. You'll get fat *if you eat too much.*

REMEMBER *Distinctive features of conditional type I*

Besonderheiten des *Conditional I*

Das *simple present* (auch die Passivform) kann nicht nur im if-Nebensatz, sondern auch im Hauptsatz verwendet werden. Solche Sätze drücken eine Tatsache oder eine allgemeingültige Aussage aus und **if** kann durch **when** oder **whenever** ausgetauscht werden.

Beispiele:

If my dog **sees** a postman, he **barks**.	**Whenever** my dog sees ...
If water **is** heated to 100 degrees Celsius, it **boils**.	**When** water is heated ...

Obwohl seltener, sind andere Verbindungen selbstverständlich möglich.

Beispiele:

If they are watching TV, I won't disturb them.	*present progressive + will-future*
If Anna has prepared a meal, we'll eat it.	*present perfect + will-future*
If that bus stops, I'm going to get on it.	*simple present + going to-future*

3 Choose the correct main clause for each conditional clause.

1. If cows listen to classical music,
2. Andy must look after his younger sister
3. If we take a taxi to the studio from Heathrow airport,
4. You get the colour green
5. If Jordan wants something,
6. If Amy knows the answer,
7. Something bad always happens
8. If you are going for a walk today,

A. he always gets it.
B. it'll costs more but we'll get there faster.
C. take an umbrella.
D. they give more milk.
F. if Dad uses my computer!
E. if you add blue to yellow.
G. if his parents go shopping together.
H. she always tells us.

4 Put the verbs in brackets in the correct tense.

1. (answer – have) I ______ these letters today if I ______ time.
2. (leave – not be) If we ______ now, we ______ late.
3. (buy – remember) Tom ______ a newspaper if he ______.
4. (you/help? – ask) ______ me if I ______ nicely?
5. (have – get) I ______ a long rest if I ______ the chance.
6. (not disturb – work) I ______ you if you ______.
7. (wash up – dry) I ______ up if you ______ the dishes.

REMEMBER *Conditional type II*

Der Sprecher hält die Bedingung für nicht real erfüllbar ***(unreal situation)***. Man darf sich aber vorstellen, was passieren könnte, wenn die Bedingung trotzdem erfüllt würde.

Beispiele:

Dick is so lazy – if he **died**, he **would be reborn** as a sofa!
If Tom **had** any sense, he **would look for** another job.
If we **ran** very quickly, we **could catch** that bus.
If I **was** a millionaire, I **would buy** you that sports car.

Das Verb im if-Nebensatz steht im *simple past*. Im Hauptsatz wird would/could + *infinitive* benutzt.

5 Put the verbs in brackets in the correct tense.

1. (go – admire) If we ______ to New York, we ______ the view from the observation platform at the top of the Empire State Building.
2. (have – not take) If you ______ a sense of humour, you ______ yourself so seriously.

3. (not be – understand) If you ______ so insensitive, you ______ my feelings better.
4. (not help – not be able to) If Jane ______ me with my maths homework, I ______ keep up in class.
5. (explain – not ask) If he ______ things more clearly, his pupils ______ so many questions.
6. (be – not complain) If Tom and Rick ______ more careful workers, their boss ______ so much.
7. (not lie – like) If Lucy ______ so much, people ______ her a lot better.
8. (find – complete) If we ______ the missing piece, we ______ this jigsaw puzzle.
9. (know – not eat) If people ______ what went into these sausages, they ______ them.

REMEMBER *Distinctive features of conditional type II*

Besonderheiten des *Conditional II*

Um ein nicht erfülltes Ereignis auszudrücken, wird häufig bei I, he, she, it (1. und 3. Person Singular) were statt was verwendet.

Bei *wh*-Fragen kann das *simple past* im if-Nebensatz und im Hauptsatz stehen, weil es sich in diesem Fall eindeutig um ein Ereignis in der Vergangenheit handelt.

Beispiele:

If I **were** Superman, I **could fly** through the sky in my underpants.

I'**d think** twice about that if I **were** you.

If you **liked** the green tie best, why **did** you **wear** the yellow one?

6 Complete each conditional clause with a suitable main clause.

1. If I were a rabbit, ______
2. If I were a crocodile, ______
3. If I were Batman, ______
4. If I were Robin Hood, ______
5. If I were a billionaire, ______
6. If I were ______
7. If you enjoyed the party so much, why ______?

REMEMBER *Conditional type III*

Der Sprecher weiß, dass die Bedingung nicht erfüllt wurde ***(past situation)***.
Beispiele:
If I **had wanted to** win the game, I **would have done** so.
If the Titanic **hadn't hit** an iceberg, it **wouldn't have** sunk.
If our ancestors **had lived** millions of years ago, they **might have hunted** dinosaurs.
Das Verb im if-Nebensatz steht im *past perfect*. Im Hauptsatz wird would/could/might + have + Partizip Perfekt benutzt.

Distinctive features of conditional type III **– Besonderheiten des *Conditional III***
Es gibt eine Ausnahme zu der Regel oben:
Im Hauptsatz kann auch would + *infinitive* stehen, wenn man ausdrücken will, was jetzt, in der Gegenwart, die Folge wäre, wenn sich die Bedingung erfüllt hätte.
Beispiel:
If my team **had won** the match, they **would** now **be** league champions.

7 Underline the correct form of the verbs in brackets.

1. I (had won/would have won) the race if I (hadn't fallen over/didn't fall over).
2. If I (had gone/went) out, I (might have missed/will miss) Isabel's call.
3. If Susan (buys/had bought) those shoes, she (might regret/would have regretted) it.
4. I (had lost/wouldn't have lost) all my money if I (hadn't betted/have betted) on that horse!
5. If I (had jumped/hadn't jumped) out of the way, I (would now be/would now have been) dead!
6. If I (hadn't bought/had bought) some food, we (would have had/wouldn't have had) nothing to eat.
7. If you (had asked/asked) Mr Shepherd, he (could help/would have helped) you.
8. If you (could answer/had answered) the question correctly, you (would have won/had to win) a million dollars.
9. If I (prepared/had prepared) for the interview, I (might have got/get) the job.
10. If Alice (played/had played) better, she (could have won/had to win).
11. If Blue Lightning (had won/wins) the race, he (would make/would have made) lots of people very happy!

1.3 *Modal auxiliaries*

REMEMBER Eigenschaften modaler Hilfsverben

Alle ***modal auxiliaries*** (modale Hilfsverben) haben die folgenden Haupteigenschaften:

- Sie werden zusammen mit einem Vollverb (ohne to) benutzt.
- Sie haben nur eine Form für alle Personen (I, you, he, she, it, we, they).
- Fragen werden durch die Umstellung von Hilfsverb und Subjekt gebildet.
- Die Verneinung *(negation)* wird meistens durch das Hinzufügen von -n't gebildet. Eine Ausnahme bildet will – won't.

Beispiele:

Josie **can** be a nuisance.
Dogs **must** remain outside.
Shall I open a window?
The world **won't** end anytime soon.
The answer **might** surprise you.
Could I help you with those bags?
You **might** win if you're very lucky.
May I ask how old you are?
I'm here now, so you **needn't** worry.
Visitors **mustn't** touch the paintings.

needn't – used to

Nur diese Formen werden zu den modalen Hilfsverben gezählt. Die anderen Formen werden wie Vollverben verwendet.

Beispiele:

He's so rich he **needn't** work.
My father **used to** work here.

Aber:

But he's bored and he need**s** a job.
Did your father **use to** work here?

1 **Look at the function and complete the sentences with a suitable modal verb. Each verb can be used more than once.**

can *may* *might* *must* *mustn't* *needn't* *should* *will*

	Function	**Example**
1.	Angebot	I ______ give you a lift to work if you want.
2.	Erlaubnis	Yes, you ______ hold my hand.
3.	höfliche Bitte	______ I sit here?
4.	Versprechen	OK, I ______ tidy up my room first thing tomorrow.
5.	Möglichkeit	The bank ______ lend me the money I need.
6.	Wahrscheinlichkeit	You ______ be tired after that long journey.
7.	Notwendigkeit	We ______ buy a new car soon.
8.	Fähigkeit	Tom ______ think and spit at the same time!
9.	Möglichkeit	I ______ go fishing tomorrow.
10.	Verbot	Passengers ______ talk to the driver.
11.	Verpflichtung	Good neighbours ______ help each other.

12.	keine Notwendigkeit	Today is a bank holiday, so I ______ go to work.
13.	Ratschlag	You ______ drive more slowly on this road.
14.	Verbot	You ______ enter Room 666.
15.	Vermutung/Vorhersage	I think the weather ______ get better soon.
16.	keine Notwendigkeit	You ______ ring the bell because they aren't in.

GOOD TO KNOW *must – have to – have got to*

Das modale Hilfsverb must kann durch die Vollverben have to und have got to ersetzt werden.

- Bei have to werden immer die Langformen benutzt.
- Bei have got to können bei Aussagesätzen die Kurzformen benutzt werden.

Beispiele:

We must wash up after meals.
We have to wash up after meals.
We've got to wash up after meals.

She must take the dog for a walk.
She has to take the dog for a walk.
She's got to take the dog for a walk.

2 **Translate these sentences with a) *have to* and b) *have got to*.**

1. Ich muss fünf Minuten warten, weil der Zug verspätet ist.
2. Ich muss morgen nicht früh aufstehen, weil ich Urlaub habe.
3. Meine Freundin sagt mir, was ich machen muss.

GOOD TO KNOW *Modal auxiliaries and their substitutes*

Einige modale Hilfsverben im Englischen (must, needn't) haben keine Vergangenheitsform. Auch die, die eine Vergangenheitsform haben (can/could, may/might, will/would, shall/should), können nur dann für die Vergangenheit benutzt werden, wenn der Sinn **unmissverständlich** ist. Sonst werden sie durch andere Verben mit einer ähnlichen Bedeutung ersetzt.

Beispiele:

We **must** find the key. → We **had to** find the key.
You **needn't** do it again. → You **didn't have to** do it again.
Jason **may** use his brother's bike. → Jason **was allowed to** use his brother's bike.

Aber:
Mike **can't** read yet. → At that time Mike **couldn't** read (yet).
I **can't** understand/help him. → I **couldn't** understand/help him.
I think he **may/might/will** come. → I thought he **might/would** come.
In diesen Beispielen ist der Vergangenheitsbezug unmissverständlich.
Hier findest du eine Übersicht über die Formen und ihre Verwendung:

Modal	Funktion	Ersatz in der Gegenwart	Ersatz in der Vergangenheit	Ersatz in der Zukunft
must	*Verpflichtung (müssen)*	has/have to has/have got to	had to	will have to
needn't	*keine Notwendigkeit (nicht brauchen)*	needn't doesn't/don't have to	didn't have to	will not/won't have to
can	*Fähigkeit (können)*	am/is/are able to	was/were able to	will be able to
can/could/may	*Erlaubnis/Bitte (dürfen)*	am/is/are allowed to	was/were allowed to	will be allowed to

3 **Complete these sentences with *can/can't, could/couldn't, must/mustn't/needn't* as appropriate.**

1. You ______ take food into the living room, it'll drive my parents crazy.
2. Would you sit down, please. I ______ see the screen with you standing in front of me.
3. When I was young I ______ run a mile in four minutes, but that's forty years ago now.
4. If your toothache doesn't go away you really ______ go and see a dentist.
5. Peter has been living in Italy for five years, so he ______ speak Italian fluently.
6. I'm going to change your bed linen this evening, so you ______ make your beds today.
7. You ______ go to the beach this afternoon so long as you tidy up your rooms first.
8. I ______ understand what the teacher was saying, so I asked her to repeat it.
9. Your daughter is too fat, Mrs Williams. I'm afraid she ______ go on a diet.
10. This interview is very important, Harry. You ______ be late this time!
11. I can order all the books you need online. You ______ go to a bookshop.

Test

1 Fill in the passive forms of the verbs in brackets.

1. Last summer my girlfriend Janet and I (show) ______ around this horrible old building by a lady guide. In the tourist brochure it (describe) ______ as the "stately home" of the Earl of Milford. Janet is an American and she loved this kind of thing.
2. First we (take) ______ around the outside of the house. So now we know when the house (build) ______ and who for and who by. Can you imagine going to your local builder and saying, "Hi, Bob. I (just/make) ______ an Earl because my wife is the King's mistress. Can you build us something with 120 rooms?" Our guide didn't tell us that, I looked it up before we came. And she didn't tell us about the whole village which (pull down) ______ to make room for these boring formal gardens.
3. Then we (lead) ______ into a big empty hall with bare walls. Our guide pointed to some empty niches around the walls and we (inform) ______ that the magnificent collection of Chinese porcelain (can/now/see) ______ at the Metropolitan Museum of Art in New York. I examined my ticket, but a trip to New York (not include) ______ in the price. (the collection/sell) ______ to the Americans?
4. Our guide told us that portraits of the family (find) ______ on the grand stairway, which we were going to (take to) ______ next. The Americans probably didn't want to buy them. As we walked up the stairs, we (stare at) ______ by the Earl's dead ancestors. The bodies of various dead animals (place) ______ at their feet. They all looked as if they (paint) ______ by a serial killer. I wanted to leave, but Janet took my hand as we (herd) ______ along a long gloomy corridor. "Gee, Frank, this is what I like about Britain – you've got so much history to be proud of." So I patted her hand and smiled and told her that Americans had some pretty good history of their own. After all, the grandson of the first Earl (shot) ______ by an American as he was having a pee behind his tent before the battle of Yorktown. And if that isn't something to be proud of, I don't know what is.

You get 1 point for each correct answer. Your points: ____ /18

2 Identify the correct type of conditional sentence.

Type 1: real situation **Type 2: unreal situation** **Type 3: past situation**

1. If I wasn't so tired, I would go jogging. Type
2. If Emma eats peanuts, her face swells and turns red. Type
3. If she needed help, we would give it. Type
4. If you believe his story, you must be mad. Type
5. If I cook the meal, you can set the table and wash up. Type
6. If I had wanted your advice, I would have asked for it. Type
7. If I hadn't gone to Chicago, I wouldn't have met Cindy. Type
8. If I were a wasp, I would sting you! Type
9. If I give up smoking, you must give it up, too. Type

You get 1 point for each correct answer. **Your points:** /9

3 Put the verb in the correct form.

1. Diana (like) ______ science fiction, so she'll love this film.
2. If I (save) ______ enough money, I could buy a moped.
3. If I (be) ______ you, I would say as little as possible.
4. If you (want) ______ the blue blouse, why did you buy the white one?
5. If you (ask) ______ me nicely, I would have told you.
6. If you (pay) ______ me £5, I would mow your lawn and trim your hedge.
7. If more cyclists (wear) ______ something bright at night, there would be fewer accidents.
8. If the cyclist (wear) ______ something bright, we would have seen him.
9. If it (be) ______ on a plate in front of him, he'll eat it.
10. If we (not move) ______, they wouldn't have seen us.
11. If you (know) ______ the correct answer, why did you still get it wrong?
12. If he (need) ______ more money, he'll have to earn it.

You get 1 point for each correct answer. **Your points:** /12

4 Rewrite the sentences using a substitute for the modal.

1. We couldn't go fishing yesterday because the weather was too rough.
2. If you have a bad toothache, you must see a dentist.
3. Sarah could already ride a pony when she was seven.
4. Slow down, there's a school ahead and you mustn't go faster than 20 mph.
5. You needn't stay at school next year if you get an apprenticeship.
6. Can I let my dog off the lead in this park?

7. The sign says that after 9 a.m. drivers must pay $2 an hour to park here.
8. Can anybody here explain Einstein's general theory of relativity?
9. The concert doesn't start for another hour, so we needn't hurry.
10. Some whales can dive to depths of 1500 metres and more.
11. Can we smoke in this part of the restaurant?

You get 1 point for each correct answer. **Your points:** ___ /11

5 Complete these sentences with a suitable modal verb from the list below.

can/could *may/might* *must/mustn't/needn't* *shall/should* *will/would* *can't/couldn't*

1. You ___ buy any wine for this evening. Alice just gave me a bottle.
2. Pete suggested meeting for lunch today, as he ___ come yesterday.
3. Dick's late. He ___ have forgotten that he had to be here by 11 o'clock.
4. I'm not sure who wrote that book, but it ___ be Charles Dickens.
5. As you've just been quite sick, you ___ not be able to go to school tomorrow.
6. ___ we invite Leo and Janice to go to Venice with us?
7. Jana's father is French, so she ___ speak French quite well.
8. You ___ smoke here. Look at that sign!
9. ___ you all sit down, please – then we can begin.
10. You really ___ talk to Margaret about it. She's really upset, you know.

You get 1 point for each correct answer. **Your points:** ___ /10

Your total points out of 60 points: ___

- More than 51? Very good.
- More than 45? Good.
- Less than 30? Have a look at the grammar pages again.
  You CAN do better.

1.4 *The past tenses*

REMEMBER Die Vergangenheitsformen im Überblick

simple past (A) Regelmäßig: Grundform des Verbs + -ed Unregelmäßig, z. B. was, sank, did, took	***past progressive (B)*** was/were + ing-Form des Verbs (Partizip Präsens)
present perfect (C) has/have + Partizip Perfekt	***present perfect progressive (D)*** has/have been + ing-Form
past perfect (E) had + Partizip Perfekt	***past perfect progressive (F)*** had been + ing-Form

1 **Identify the tenses (A-F above) in the following sentences.**

1. My parents have lived in several countries.
2. They have travelled a lot.
3. They have been living in Germany since 1992.
4. They lived in Canada before that.
5. They had been living there for 2 years (when I was born).
6. My father had gone there to work for his company.
7. My parents both grew up in Liverpool.
8. My father worked for a shipping company in Liverpool.
9. My mother was working in a hotel at that time.
10. She was a receptionist there and had a room at the hotel.
11. My father was living in a small flat at the time.
12. They met at a Beatles concert and married in 1978.

2 **Complete the sentences using an appropriate tense.**

1. Last week Carol (back out of) ______ a parking space when she (run into) ______ a tree and damaged her car.
2. She (not look) ______ behind her.
3. She (take) ______ her car to the garage after the accident.
4. A mechanic (work) ______ on it for three days now.
5. He (replace) ______ all the damaged parts.

REMEMBER *Simple past and past progressive*

Das *simple past* und das *past progressive* treten oft zusammen auf. Das *past progressive* drückt aus, dass ein Vorgang gerade ablief, als etwas Neues geschah.
Beispiel: When I first **saw** her, Jane **was sitting** alone **drinking** a coffee.
Bei einer Wiederholung einer Zeitform in einem Satz muss man das Hilfsverb nicht wiederholen.

3 Complete these sentences with the simple past or past progressive form of the verbs.

1. (feel – arrive) We ______ tired and hungry when the coach finally ______ at our hotel.
2. (sit – read – start) Colin ______ right next to me ______ his programme when the concert ______.
3. (drive – slow down – happen) We ______ past the cinema and just ______ when the accident ______.
4. (wake up – be – run – drip) I ______ suddenly. The window ______ open and the rain ______ down the wall and ______ onto my bed.
5. (know – walk – go) I ______ she ______ from the station so I ______ to meet her.
6. (arrive – eat – have – watch) When I ______ at the Barclays', they ______ a meal, ______ an argument, and ______ TV at the same time.
7. (cut – break down) I ______ the grass when the lawnmower ______.

REMEMBER *Present perfect and simple past*

Das *present perfect* drückt aus, dass ...
- eine Handlung in der Vergangenheit begonnen hat und noch nicht abgeschlossen ist oder
- eine Handlung in der Vergangenheit Auswirkung auf die Gegenwart hat bzw. ein Resultat vorliegt.

Der Zeitpunkt der Handlung wird nicht weiter bestimmt. Das *simple past* bezieht sich dagegen immer auf einen spezifischen Zeitpunkt in der Vergangenheit.
Beispiele:
Mr and Mrs Watson **have lived** here for six years. They **moved** here six years ago.
Jim **has cut** his foot badly. He **stepped** onto a broken bottle on the beach.
Have you seen my keys anywhere? I can't find them.

4 Use the words below to make either a statement or a question. Use the simple past or the present perfect.

EXAMPLE

anybody | *call* | *when I* | *be out?*

Did anybody call when I was out?

1. *my Grandma* | *never drive a car*
2. *you* | *ever see the Golden Temple in Amritsar?*
3. *you* | *visit Rome* | *when you* | *be in Italy last summer?*
4. *I* | *lose my car key somewhere*
5. *you* | *ever have a tetanus injection?*
6. *when you* | *have your last tetanus injection?*
7. *you* | *find your coat* | *yet?*
8. *where you* | *find your coat?*

5 Complete the dialogue with the correct tenses of the verbs.

1. Sheila: Hello, Carol. (you/talk to) ________ Dave Chambers yet?
2. Carol: Yes, Dave and I (have) ________ a meeting yesterday afternoon. He (tell) ________ me about the CeBIT trade fair in Hannover.
3. Sheila: Oh, did he? Our company (not attend) ________ the fair for five or six years, and in fact I (never be) ________ there at all.
4. Carol: Yes, Dave and I (discuss) ________ that at our meeting. I (send) ________ you an e-mail with the details later that afternoon.
5. Sheila: Yes, thank you. I (just/read) ________ it.
6. Carol: Good. Yesterday I (give) ________ your secretary a list of our customers in Germany. (you/have) ________ a chance to look through it yet?
7. Sheila: Not yet, I'm afraid. Our computer network (crash) ________ again and my secretary (not be able to) ________ print it out yet.

REMEMBER *Present perfect progressive*

Das *present perfect progressive* wird benutzt für Situationen oder Handlungen, die in der Vergangenheit angefangen haben und noch andauern oder deren Wirkung noch andauert. Der Ablauf oder die Dauer der Handlung wird betont.

Beispiele:

You've been talking in your sleep again.

I hope you **haven't been waiting** long.

I'm afraid the children are rather dirty – **they've been playing** out in the woods.

6 **Complete the sentences with the present perfect progressive forms of a suitable verb.**

avoid *dream* *promise* *read* *steal* *work*

1. Dad ______ in the garden for three hours.
2. You ______ to decorate the flat ever since we moved here.
3. Tim ______ that book for two months.
4. Carol ______ of a holiday in Tahiti since she was a little girl.
5. Somebody in the office ______ money for several weeks now.
6. People in the office ______ me since I married the boss's daughter!

7 **Complete the dialogue with either the present perfect simple or present perfect progressive form of the verbs.**

1. Ms Cox: Hello, Mr Hill and welcome back. Your friend, Mr Wells (call) ______ several times this morning.
2. Mr Hill: (he/leave) ______ a message?
3. Ms Cox: No, he hasn't, but he (give) ______ me a phone number.
4. Dick Hill: Hello, Tom. (you/try) ______ to reach me?
5. Tom Wells: Yes. (I/phone) ______ your office all week! Where (you/be) ______?
6. Dick Hill: (I/spend) ______ the last two weeks in Asia. (I/visit) ______ our factories there. Why? What's up?
7. Tom Wells: (you/not/hear) ______ the news yet?
8. Dick Hill: No. What (happen) ______?
9. Tom Wells: My firm (just/buy) ______ your firm. Nobody (see) ______ your boss for several days. Everybody thinks that he (already/leave) ______ the firm. And my boss (interview) ______ people for your job!

REMEMBER *Past perfect progressive*

Diese Zeitform tritt oft zusammen mit dem *simple past* auf.

Beispiele:

The police soon **found** the thief. He **had been hiding** in a cupboard.

I **had been working** there for ten years before they **gave** me a pay rise.

8 Complete the text with an appropriate verb form.

1. Dr Merryweather and his wife (often/visit) __________ Europe. They (take) __________ their holidays in Europe for fifteen years now. In all this time they (tour) __________ several countries: Britain, France, Italy, Spain, Germany and Austria. But until last year they (never/stay) __________ in any country longer than a couple of days.

2. Last summer they (spend) __________ their entire summer holiday in Britain. And they (not just stay) __________ in London this time, either.
3. They (choose) __________ a comfortable hotel in Dover, (hire) __________ a car and (drive) __________ along the south coast of England. They (stop) __________ at almost every little fishing village on the coast. They (look for) __________ a typical English cottage in a quiet, peaceful village.

4. Dr Merryweather and his wife (both/retire) __________ at the beginning of that year and (sell) __________ their dental practice in Detroit. They (live) __________ in a city-centre apartment in Detroit for over thirty years. They (not want to) __________ spend their retirement in a big city like Detroit; it (be) __________ time for a change.
5. They (buy) __________ an old fisherman's cottage in Polperro which they (now/extend) __________ and (modernize) __________ .

1.5 *The future tenses*

REMEMBER *Simple present* und Futur

Das *simple present* wird auch in Nebensätzen der Zeit verwendet, wenn der Hauptsatz das *will-future* oder *going to-future* benutzt. Solche Nebensätze werden durch Verbindungswörter *(conjunctions)* eingeleitet, z. B.:
as soon as, immediately, before, until/till, unless, if, when, by the time

Achtung: if = etwas wird vielleicht geschehen
when = etwas wird bestimmt geschehen

Beispiele:
They'll call us **as soon as** they hear anything.
Who is going to tell him the bad news **when** he asks?
Please wait here **until** I come.
I'm not going to clean the house **before** they arrive – they're bringing their dog.
We will leave **unless** she asks us to stay.

1 **What do these expressions mean in German?**
Match the English and the German expressions.

1. as soon as
2. before
3. if
4. until/till
5. when
6. unless

A. vor; bevor
B. als, wenn
C. außer wenn, es sei denn
D. sobald
E. wenn, falls; ob
F. bis

2 **Complete these sentences with a suitable conjunction.**

unless *when/as soon as* *if* *when* *if* *when/as soon as*
unless *is* *when/as soon as*

1. ______ Mr James calls, I'll see him at once.
2. Please bring me their fax ______ it arrives.
3. We'll take a taxi from the airport ______ we arrive.
4. We'll only take a taxi from the airport ______ we're short of time.
5. We won't take a taxi from the airport ______ we're short of time.
6. She'll call us ______ she arrives at the station.
7. She won't call us ______ something goes wrong.
8. We'll arrange another meeting ______ you're ill.
9. We'll arrange another meeting ______ you're feeling better.

REMEMBER *Present with future meaning*

Beide Gegenwartsformen können mit einer Zeitangabe zukünftige Ereignisse ausdrücken, die fest geplant oder festgelegt sind. Dabei wird das *simple present* für Ereignisse benutzt, die nach einem von außen festgelegten Zeitplan ablaufen (Kino, Schule, öffentliche Verkehrsmittel usw.), das *present progressive* dagegen für persönliche Vereinbarungen, Pläne und Termine. Wie immer ist es die Sicht des Sprechers, die die Wahl der Zeiten bestimmt.

Beispiele:

Your train **arrives** at Paddington station at 3.45 p.m. You **have** twenty-six minutes before your connection **leaves**. It **leaves** from platform 17 at 4.11 p.m.

School **starts** on August 17th, but we're only **flying back** from Delhi on 16th, and our plane **doesn't land** in Frankfurt till 6 p.m. So I'm going to be a bit tired the next day.

I'**m seeing** Jane tomorrow. We'**re planning to go** to the States in the autumn. We'**re flying** to San Francisco and **staying** with her cousin for a few days before we **go** on to LA and southern California.

3 **Translate the following sentences into English. Use the simple present.**

1. Hier ist Ihr Zeitplan[1] für die nächsten drei Tage, Frau[2] Chapman.
2. Ihr Zug kommt in King's Cross in London um 6.25 Uhr[3] an.
3. Ihr Flug ist erst um 8.50 Uhr.
4. Sie haben also genug Zeit für ein schnelles Frühstück und die Fahrt nach Heathrow Airport.
5. Das Flugzeug macht einen kurzen Halt in New York und fliegt dann weiter nach Orlando.
6. Sie holen Ihr Auto am Ajax-Schalter ab, fahren nach St Petersburg und checken sich im Marryat Hotel ein.
7. Eine Straßenkarte befindet sich im Handschuhfach[4].
8. Ihr erstes Treffen ist am nächsten Vormittag um 10.30 Uhr.
9. Hier ist die Adresse.
10. Ihr nächstes Treffen ist erst um 18.30 Uhr[5], Sie haben also eine Menge Zeit.

[1] schedule, [2] Ms (pronounced 'Miz'), [3] a.m., [4] glove compartment, [5] p.m.

4 **Pre-listening task: Look at the photo on the following page.**

What information does it give you about the listening text on the CD?

The building is ______ and it's in ______.

So the listening text on the CD will probably be about ______.

5 Listen to the plans for the class trip to London and fill in the details of the schedule. Track 1

Times	Places	Activities
9.15 a.m.	pick up outside hotel	

REMEMBER *Will-future and going to-future*

Das ***will-future*** benutzt man
- bei einem spontanen Entschluss,
- bei Vermutungen (z. B. nach den Verben to think, to be sure, to hope, to promise),
- bei allgemeinen Voraussagen.

Beispiele:
Tom, I often feel lonely. – OK, Janet. **I'll buy** you a dog.
I'm seeing Mr Jones tomorrow. **I'll talk** to him about it then.
Our team is playing well. I'm sure they**'ll win** the cup this year.
Rain **will spread** over northern Germany during the night.

Das ***going to-future*** benutzt man,
- wenn eine Absicht/Entscheidung schon feststeht (= schon gefasste Absicht),
- wenn etwas offensichtlich kurz bevorsteht (= Unmittelbarkeit).

In beiden Fällen stehen die Gründe der Handlung bzw. des Ereignisses im Vordergrund. Die Gründe können eine feste Absicht *(intention)* oder äußere Ursachen *(imminence)* sein.

Beispiele:
I've talked to Sally. **She's going to drive** us home.
This can't go on. **I'm going to talk** to your parents about your behaviour.
The taxi driver hasn't seen us. **She isn't going to stop**.
It looks as if **it's going to rain**.
I think **I'm going to be sick**.

Ob man will oder going to benutzt, ist also oft eine subjektive Entscheidung.

Beispiele:

I'm sure **it will rain** this afternoon.	(inneres Gefühl wird betont)
It looks as if **it's going to rain** this afternoon.	(äußere Indizien werden betont)

Wenn du unsicher bist, welche der beiden Zukunftsformen du verwenden sollst, dann wähle will, weil es neutraler ist.

6 ***Will*** **or** ***going to*****? Which is most suitable in these situations?**

1. I haven't got a car. – That's OK. (I/give) __________ you a lift.
2. We don't need the bus. Carol (give) __________ us a lift.
3. What's this new program like? – It's terrific! Come on, (I/show) __________ you.
4. Brrr! It's cold in here! – Yes, it is, isn't it. (I/turn) __________ the heating up.
5. I'm expecting a visitor later. So (I/turn) __________ the heating up a little.
6. I've got to cut the grass this afternoon. (you/help) __________ me?

7. Joe, Dad asked you to help him cut the grass. (you/do) ______ that?
8. I'm going out for an hour or two. (I/bring back) ______ a couple of pizzas.
9. John wants to go shopping tomorrow. (He/buy) ______ a new suit.
10. Is Alice coming to our party or not? – I don't know. (I/call) ______ her and ask.
11. I don't know if Alice is coming to our party. (I/call) ______ her this afternoon anyway, so I'll ask her.

7 Translate these sentences into English, using the will-future or the going to-future as appropriate. Sometimes you can use either.

1. Der Junge da wird gleich vom Fahrrad fallen!
2. Sei vorsichtig oder du wirst dich verletzen!
3. Es wird in einer Stunde dunkel.
4. Ich bin sicher, dass Tom dort sein wird.
5. Es wird morgen schneien.
6. Wir werden morgen sehr beschäftigt sein.
7. Ich habe Hunger. Ich mache mir ein Sandwich.
8. Jane wird das Essen für unsere Party kaufen.
9. Wir werden an der nächsten Tankstelle[1] halten.
10. Ich verspreche, dass ich's nicht wieder mache.

[1] filling station

REMEMBER *Future progressive*

Das *future progressive* wird mit will be + ing-Form gebildet. Es wird verwendet

- für einen Vorgang, der zu einem bestimmten Zeitpunkt in der Zukunft im Gange sein wird,
- für zukünftige Vorgänge (oft in Zusammenhang mit anyway), die sowieso geschehen werden,
- um höflich nach einem zukünftigen Vorhaben zu fragen. Es hört sich im Englischen weniger bestimmend an, es wirkt eher beiläufig.

Beispiele:
This time tomorrow **we'll be sitting** on the plane to Jamaica.
I'll take your empty bottles back. **I'll be going** to the supermarket anyway.
Will your secretary **be travelling** with you this time, too, Mr Beasley?

Man kann mit dem *future progressive* auch eher beiläufig und unaufdringlich um einen Gefallen bitten, an etwas erinnern oder taktvoll Kritik üben.

Beispiele:
I need some stamps. **Will you be going** past the post office by any chance?
Hello, Fred. **Will you be bringing** my lawnmower back soon? My lawn needs it.
Your report isn't very clear. But **you'll be rewriting** it, won't you?

8 What would you say in these situations? Use the future progressive.

1. Es hat gestern geregnet und es regnet heute immer noch. Überlege, ob es morgen um die gleiche Zeit immer noch regnen wird. (I wonder if ...?)
2. Du fragst deine Schwester, ob sie heute Nachmittag eventuell Tennis spielt.
3. Du fragst den Trainer, wo das Team wohl am nächsten Sonntag spielen wird.
4. Du sagst deinen Eltern, dass du heute Abend zu Hause bleiben wirst.
5. Ein Freund/Eine Freundin ruft an und will um 17.30 vorbei kommen. Er/Sie soll eine halbe Stunde später kommen, weil du um diese Zeit noch deine Hausaufgaben machen wirst.
6. Eine Tante ruft an und kündigt ihren baldigen Besuch an. Du fragst sie, wann sie vorhat zu kommen.
7. Du und ein Freund/eine Freundin sind zum Essen eingeladen. Du bist nicht sicher, was du anziehen sollst und fragst deinen Freund/deine Freundin, was er/sie tragen wird.
8. Du verabredest dich mit einem Freund/einer Freundin. Ihr wollt euch im Stadtzentrum treffen. Du sagst, dass du vor dem Kino warten wirst.
9. Du willst nach Berlin reisen. Dein Freund/deine Freundin hat gefragt, mit wem du zusammen reisen wirst. Du sagst, du wirst mit drei Freunden fahren.

REMEMBER *Future perfect (simple)*

Das *future perfect (simple form)* wird so gebildet: will have + Partizip Perfekt.
Mit dieser Form der Zukunft kann man ausdrücken, was zu einem bestimmten Zeitpunkt in der Zukunft abgeschlossen oder nicht abgeschlossen sein wird.
Beispiel:
We're late! By the time we get home the film **will have ended**.
Beachte: Das *future perfect* wird häufig mit yet oder by now benutzt. Dann drückt es die Wahrscheinlichkeit aus, dass etwas in der Gegenwart abgeschlossen oder nicht abgeschlossen ist.
Beispiel:
It's only 8 a.m. in Florida. They **won't have started** work yet.

9 Complete these sentences using the future perfect.

1. I (do) ________ it by the time you return.
2. I'm sure the police (catch) ________ the bank robbers by tomorrow.
3. I expect you (hear) ________ from him by the end of the week.
4. The Robinsons (sell) ________ their house by now.
5. There's still time. The concert (not start) ________ yet.
6. You needn't hurry. The train (not arrive) ________ yet.
7. Jane doesn't know. Pete (not speak to) ________ her yet.

1.6 *Reported speech*

REMEMBER

In der indirekten Rede *(indirect speech/reported speech)* berichtet man darüber, was jemand sagt. Der Bericht wird mit Verben wie say, think, tell, ask eingeleitet. Steht das einleitende Verb in der Gegenwart, haben die Verben im indirekten Satz die gleiche Zeitform wie in der direkten Rede.

Beispiel:

Sandra: I **love** shopping. = Sandra says (that) she **loves** shopping.

Achtung:

- Im Englischen steht vor der indirekten Rede kein Komma.
- Die Konjunktion that kann man oft weglassen.

Steht das einleitende Verb des indirekten Satzes in einem ***past tense***, werden die Zeitformen der direkten Rede um eine Zeitstufe weiter in die Vergangenheit gesetzt *(backshift).* Bei Sätzen mit Nebensätzen wird allerdings meist nur der Hauptsatz verschoben.

Beispiele:

Jim:	I **love** windsurfing.	→	Jim told us he **loved** windsurfing.
Ann:	We**'re feeling** tired.	→	Ann admitted they **were feeling** tired.
Paula:	Tom **didn't call**.	→	Paula said Tom **hadn't called**.
Bill:	My goldfish **has died**.	→	Bill told us his goldfish **had died**.
Carol:	When **can** you come?	→	Carol asked when I **could** come.
Ron:	When I heard Harry had broken his leg, I was really mad at him.	→	Ron told me that he **had been** really mad at Harry when he heard he had broken his leg.

Achtung:

Das ***past perfect*** sowie would, could, should und might bleiben unverändert.

Beispiele:

Bob: I **couldn't** go on the trip because I **had broken** my leg.

Bob explained that he **couldn't** go on the trip because he **had broken** his leg.

Außer den Personalpronomen müssen Zeit- und manchmal auch Ortsangaben angepasst werden, z. B.:

direct speech	***indirect speech***
today	that (same) day
yesterday	the day before/the previous day
the day before yesterday	two days before/previously
tomorrow	the next/following day
this week/month/year/...	that week/month/year/...
next week/month/year/Sunday/...	the following week/month/Sunday/...
here	where he/she was standing

Da die indirekte Rede ein Bericht ist, kann man die Sätze der direkten Rede (z. B. bei einem Dialog) auch logisch miteinander verknüpfen.
Beispiele: So she answered ... Then he said ... Finally he admitted ...

1 Complete the sentences.

EXAMPLE

Dave: Who won the darts match last Thursday?
Dave asked *who had won the darts match the previous Thursday.*

1. Bill: I don't want to visit any museums this weekend.
   Bill said ______.
2. Chris: I was sleeping when the fire started.
   Chris told us ______ when the fire started.
3. Joe: Let's ride our bikes to the beach after school tomorrow.
   Joe suggested ______.
4. Mark: When we discovered that Ben had lied to us, we were very angry.
   Mark explained ______
5. Carol: George, when would it be convenient for you to visit?
   Carol asked George when it ______ to visit.
6. Mike: I'm going to write some letters before I go out.
   Mike told ______.

2 Rewrite these sentences as direct speech.

1. Alex told me that his grandfather kept rabbits in his garden shed.
   Alex: My grandfather ______.
2. Linda explained that she had been ill the day before and hadn't gone to work.
   Linda: I ______.
3. Keith admitted that he hadn't prepared for the test on the following day.
   Keith: I ______.
4. Mr Noble confided that business hadn't been very good that month.
   Mr Noble: Business ______.

REMEMBER *Questions in reported speech*

Wenn die direkte Rede kein Fragewort enthält, muss man entweder **if** oder **whether** benutzen:

Beispiele:

Alice: Would you like a cup of tea? = Alice asked (me) **if** I would like a cup of tea.

Alice: Do you take sugar? = She wanted to know **if/whether** I took sugar.

Hinweis: Beachte die Bildung von höflichen Bitten und Aufforderungen, Befehlen und Verboten sowie Warnungen.

Beispiele:

Bill: Please tidy up your room. → Bill **asked me to** tidy up my room.

Tom: Don't touch my things! → Bill **told me not to** touch his things.

Andy: Don't get too near the edge of the cliff! → Andy **warned us not to** get too near the edge of the cliff.

3 Rewrite this dialogue as reported speech.

You can leave out the underlined words.

1. Jim: Have you been shopping, Jane?
2. Jane: Yes. Will you help me carry some bags from my car, please?
3. Jim: OK. Where should I take them?
4. Jane: Just put them on the kitchen counter.
5. Jim: Can I help you put everything away?
6. Jane: Do you know where it all goes?
7. Jim: Of course. The tins go in the cupboard and everything else goes in the fridge.
8. Jane: Please leave it. I've got my own system and you'll just get everything muddled up.

4 Rewrite these questions as reported speech.

1. Jessica: Is anybody feeling hungry?
   Jessica asked ______.
2. Paul: Yes. Have you got any sandwiches?
   Paul said he was and ______.
3. Jessica: Yes. I've got BLT sandwiches and tuna fish sandwiches.
   Jessica said she ______.
4. Paul: What's a BLT sandwich?
   Paul wanted to know ______.
5. Jessica: It's a sandwich with bacon, lettuce and tomato. Do you want one?
   Jessica told him ______.

Test

1 These future expressions are missing from the following text.
Where do they go? The first one is done for you.

A will be
B take over
C will have come
D it'll be too late
E was I going to do
F will soon be over
G I'd be flying
H are we going to wait
I will drive
J ~~we'll have been watching~~
K would we all be
L They'll wait
M will open
N We're going to lock
O will land
P will be waiting
Q arrives
R will come
S will ring
T I'll go crazy
U he'll be depositing
V will have landed

There were three of us in the little hotel room. Anton stood by the window. He put down the binoculars and looked at his watch. "In exactly five minutes (1) J this bank for four days! How much longer (2) ___ ! The routine never varies. The manager (3) ___ at exactly 8.15. That's in seven minutes. By 8.25 all the staff (4) ___ . The bank (5) ___ for business at 8.30 and their first customers (6) ___ the local shopkeepers wanting small change." Annette stood up. "Just one more day in this room and (7) ___ !" I decided to end their impatience. "The call (8) ___ in the next few minutes", I said. "The waiting (9) ___ ."

Meanwhile the fourth member of our team was watching a small landing strip at a farm just outside the town. We're certain, I thought, that today is when a small plane (10) ___ at around 8.20. It's bringing a diamond smuggler. Two men (11) ___ for him in a blue van and (12) ___ him to the bank opposite our hotel. (13) ___ outside while he goes in and asks to see his deposit box. When we're sure that he's on his way we intend to (14) ___ the bank. (15) ___ the staff in a storeroom and take their places. And when our smuggler opens his deposit box, (16) ___ the diamonds with us. "The manager arrived seven minutes ago," Anton told us. "If that phone doesn't ring soon, (17) ___ ." I looked at my watch: 8.22. The smuggler's plane (18) ___ by now, I thought. "Get ready. The phone (19) ___ in the next minute or two," I told them. Where (20) ___ this time tomorrow, I wondered. Perhaps (21) ___ to an island paradise. My share of the diamonds was 6 million U.S. dollars. What (22) ___ with so much money? And then the phone by the bed rang. I shouldn't have picked it up. Because that was when the dream ended and the nightmare began.

You get 1 point for each correct answer. **Your points:** ___ /21

2 Complete this text with the past forms of the verbs.

Inspector Boston and the two soldiers (walk) ______ through the jungle for three hours when they (find) ______ the body. They (hear) ______ some crows and (leave) ______ the path to investigate. They (make) ______ lots of noise as they (cut) ______ their way through the undergrowth and the crows (fly off) ______ in an angry flock and (reveal) ______ what they (eat) ______. It (once/be) ______ a man. Inspector Boston (wave) ______ away the countless flies with one hand and (hold) ______ a handkerchief to his nose with the other as he (examine) ______ the body carefully. On discovering the body, Sergeant Forbes (turn away) ______ and (be) ______ sick behind a bush covered with blood-red blossoms. Meanwhile Corporal Lazenby (take off) ______ her backpack and (talk) ______ into her radiophone. "I'm afraid that I (not/be able to) ______ reach headquarters, sir," she said. "That's a pity," Boston replied, "because we're in great danger and we need their help – and pretty damn quick, too!" Sergeant Forbes (move) ______ closer to Inspector Boston, he (try) ______ very hard not to look at the body at Boston's feet. "The bastards who (do) ______ this – they (watch) ______ us since we (enter) ______ the forest, haven't they? They (know) ______ we (come) ______!" Corporal Lazenby looked up. She (search) ______ through her open backpack. "Here. You'll need this," she (say) ______ as she (throw) ______ something heavy towards Boston. He (catch) ______ it in one hand. It (be) ______ a powerful automatic pistol.

You get 1 point for each correct answer. **Your points:** ______ /30

3 Rewrite the following sentences as reported speech. Use an appropriate reporting verb.

1. Charles: "I often take the dog for a walk in the park."
2. Ted: "Everybody must have a ticket before we get on the train tomorrow morning."
3. Tina: "I'm sorry, but I won't be able to go on the class trip next Friday."
4. Susan: "I'm not very hungry because I ate a big meal only an hour ago."
5. Ian: "I tried to talk to Alan yesterday, but he didn't listen."

You get 2 points for each correct sentence. **Your points:** ______ /10

4 Rewrite the following sentences as reported speech. Use the reporting verbs below.

asked *told* *warned* *reminded*

1. Mrs Fox to her daughter: “Take your little brother to the beach with you and your friends”.
2. Mr Oliver to his children: “Come with me. I want a word with both of you.”
3. Susan to her friend: “Please help me clear the table and wash up.”
4. Ms Thomson to boy: “Why didn’t you tell me this before?”
5. Mark to Sheila: “Open the box carefully or the hamster will escape.”
6. Dentist to nurse: “How many people are waiting outside?”
7. Mrs Wood to Mr Wood: “Don’t forget your coat when we leave the restaurant.”
8. Mr Watson to Ms Wood: “Can you take these letters to the post office on your way home, please?”
9. Waitress to the Woods: “Did you enjoy your meal?”

You get 2 points for each correct answer. **Your points:** /18

5 Rewrite this dialogue as reported speech.

1. Mrs Fox: “Where’s this morning’s newspaper? Have you seen it?”
2. Mr Fox: “I’m reading it. I’ll be finished soon.”
3. Mrs Fox: “Have you read the part with the TV programmes?”
4. Mr Fox: “Are we going out tonight?”
5. Mrs Fox: “I don’t want to go out this evening. There’s a good film on TV.”
6. Mr Fox: “What’s the name of the film? Do I know it?”
7. Mrs Fox: “It’s a love story. You won’t like it.”
8. Mr Fox: “OK. You stay in and watch the film.”
9. Mrs Fox: “What will you do? Are you going to go to the pub?”

You get 2 points for each correct sentence. **Your points:** /18

Your total points out of 97 points:

- More than 83? Very good.
- More than 73? Good.
- Less than 49? Have a look at the grammar pages again.
  You CAN do better.

1.7 *Infinitive and gerund constructions*

REMEMBER

Die folgenden Infinitiv-Wendungen ohne to *(bare infinitive)* kennst du längst:

- nach modalen Hilfsverben wie will, must, can, usw.: He can run really fast.
- nach einer Verneinung mit don't: Don't touch that wire!
- nach Let's: Let's go to the beach this afternoon.
- nach help: I've just been helping her pack.

Diese Wendungen sind dir vielleicht nicht so bekannt:

- nach **let** + Objekt = etwas zulassen/erlauben
- nach **make** + Objekt = etwas erzwingen
- nach **have** + Objekt = etwas veranlassen
- nach **had better** (you'd better ...) = sollte, **would rather** (we'd rather ...) = möchte lieber, **would** = pflegte ... zu (eher Schriftsprache)
- nach einer betonten Form von **do**

Beispiele:

Dad often **lets** me borrow the car.
I **made** them stop the film.
Lord Digby **has** his lawns cut by a team of gardeners.
I'**d rather** watch the film on Channel 4.
My wife really **does** think you are an idiot.
He was a young man then and **would** go out every evening he could.

1 **Translate these sentences into English using one of the infinitive constructions indicated above.**

1. Das schlechte Wetter zwang uns, viel langsamer zu fahren.
2. Heute erlaubten wir unseren beiden Söhnen, eine Mahlzeit zu kochen.
3. Es ist zu spät für den Bus - wir sollten lieber ein Taxi bestellen.
4. Wir möchten lieber den Zoo statt das Museum besuchen.
5. Wir hoffen wirklich, dass Sie uns wieder besuchen werden.
6. Ich half Carla nach dem Essen abzuwaschen.

REMEMBER *Bare infinitive and -ing form*

Verben des Wahrnehmens und Beobachtens sind: see, notice, watch, hear, feel, smell. Diese Verben können entweder mit einem Infinitiv ohne to *(bare infinitive)* oder mit einer ing-Form benutzt werden.

Es gelten die üblichen Aspekt-Regeln: bei der ing-Form wird der Ablauf *(action in progress)*, beim Infinitiv die bloße Tatsache der Handlung *(completed action)* betont. Je nach konkreter Situation ist die Wahl des Aspekts jedoch häufig frei.

Beispiele:

I heard her open the door. (Man hört die Tür einfach aufgehen.)

I heard her opening the door. (Man hört das Knarren und Knirschen ...)

She felt something slimy touch her leg. (Sie fühlt eine flüchtige Berührung.)

She felt something slimy touching her leg. (Die Berührung ist nicht mehr flüchtig ...)

2 Complete the text with an appropriate verb form.

1. I (have) ______ a shower when I (hear) ______ somebody (knock) ______ on the door.
2. I (get out) ______ of the shower, (go) ______ into the living room and (look) ______ out of the window.
3. I (see) ______ a woman (put) ______ a leaflet in my letterbox.
4. She (look) ______ towards the window and I (notice) ______ her (make) ______ a call on her mobile phone.
5. A few minutes later, a police car (stop) ______ next to the woman.
6. I (see) ______ her (point) ______ to my window.
7. Two police officers (get) ______ out of the car and (walk) ______ up my path!
8. When I (hear) ______ my doorbell (ring) ______ I (open) ______ the door.
9. I (watch) ______ their mouths (open) ______ in surprise.
10. And then I (realize) ______ that I (not wear) ______ any clothes!
11. I (feel) ______ my face (turn) ______ bright red!

REMEMBER *To-infinitive and gerund with different meanings*

Nach den Verben stop, try, remember, forget, regret sind *to*-Infinitiv oder Gerundium möglich. Allerdings ist die Bedeutung anders.

Beispiele:

I regret to say ...	→	Ich bedaure es, sagen zu müssen ...
I regret saying ...	→	Ich bedaure es, gesagt zu haben ...
He stopped smoking.	→	Er hörte auf zu rauchen.
He stopped to smoke.	→	Er hielt an, um zu rauchen.

3 **Match the verb construction with the meaning in German.**

1. forget + *to*-infinitive
2. forget + gerund
3. try + *to*-infinitive
4. try + gerund
5. stop + *to*-infinitive
6. stop + gerund
7. remember + *to*-infinitive
8. remember + gerund

A. kurz anhalten, um etwas anderes zu tun
B. versuchen, etwas zu tun
C. aufhören, etwas zu tun
D. sich erinnern, etwas getan zu haben
E. vergessen, etwas zu tun
F. daran denken, etwas zu tun
G. vergessen, dass man etwas schon getan hat
H. etwas ausprobieren

4 **Translate these sentences into English.**

1. Ich hielt am Kiosk an, um eine Zeitung zu kaufen.
2. Er hörte auf zu atmen.
3. Ted strengte sich an, das Spiel zu gewinnen.
4. Ich habe versucht, mit ihm zu reden, aber es brachte nichts.
5. Sie erinnerte sich, einen Mann gesehen zu haben.
6. Sie dachte daran, ihren Schirm mitzunehmen.
7. Wir haben vergessen, Brot zu kaufen.
8. Sie hat schon vergessen, mit uns gesprochen zu haben.

REMEMBER *To-infinitive constructions*

Der Infinitiv mit to steht ...

- nach den Fragewörtern how, who, what, where, when, which,
- nach einem Adjektiv,
- nach for + Objekt.

Beispiele:

I don't know **where to look** or **who to ask**.
They **were ready to try** but **too tired to succeed**.
The book is **suitable for** a child **to read**.

5 **Complete these sentences with the infinitive form of a suitable verb.**

play *drive* *finish* *get to* *know* *lean* *like*
make *read* *see* *stop* *use* *wear* *learn*

1. We'll wait for you ____________ your meal and then we can all go shopping.
2. I'm afraid Ms Walsh is too busy ____________ you now. Please come back in an hour or so.

3. I can't understand Jim's note because his handwriting is too difficult ______.
4. Excuse me. Can you tell me how ______ the bus station, please?
5. Janet just isn't good enough ______ in the basketball team.
6. I don't know how ______ a car.
7. I'm not sure which tie ______ for the interview.
8. Would you please show me how ______ this software?
9. Chinese isn't an easy language ______.
10. It's important for a cook ______ about vitamins and calories.
11. Mr Digby is an unpleasant person and impossible ______.
12. It is dangerous ______ out of the window when the train is moving.
13. The trouble with Fred is he just doesn't know when ______.
14. It was a chance for them ______ a lot of money.

REMEMBER *More to-infinitive constructions*

Mit dem *to*-Infinitiv kann man einen Zweck ausdrücken. Das Wort to ist hier ein Teil der Wendung in order to (= um ... zu).

Beispiele:

They interrupted the programme **to make** an important announcement.

We stopped at a supermarket **to buy** some food.

Man kann den *to*-Infinitiv anstelle eines umständlichen Relativsatzes verwenden.

Beispiele:

He hasn't got anybody **that he can** play with. = He hasn't got anybody **to** play with.

Paul is a useful person **who you should** know. = Paul is a useful person **to** know.

6 **Rewrite these sentences using an infinitive.**

EXAMPLE

We need volunteers who can help with our theatre production.

We need volunteers to help with our theatre production.

1. Miss Hardy was the only person from the office who congratulated me on my promotion.
2. I went into the house in order to see if everything was all right.
3. Armstrong was the first man who walked on the moon.
4. If you enjoy horror films, "Glibberspawn" is a film you should watch.
5. I thought you would be the last person who would help me.
6. I don't know anybody that I could talk to.
7. Children need people that they can look up to.

1.8 *Participles*

REMEMBER

Es gibt zwei Arten von Partizipien:

- Das Partizip Präsens hat die -ing-Form, z. B.: exciting, seeing, usw.
- Das Partizip Perfekt hat die 3. Form des Verbs, z. B.: talked, worried, told, usw.

Beide Partizipien können als Adjektive benutzt werden.

Beispiele:

Talking computers will soon be quite common.

Harry has got a **broken** heart.

Tipp zur Unterscheidung der Partizipien:

Du möchtest ein Partizip in einem englischen Satz als Adjektiv benutzen, aber du bist nicht sicher, welche Art richtig ist. Formuliere den Satz zuerst auf Deutsch. Du kannst das Partizip Präsens im Deutschen an der Endung *-end* erkennen, z. B.: Der Arzt verband die blutende Wunde. Dann wird auch im Englischen das Partizip Präsens verwendet (= ... the bleeding wound).

Sonst wird das Partizip Perfekt verwendet.

Beispiel:

Wir mussten über umgefallene Bäume klettern. (= ... fallen trees)

1 Complete the sentences with the correct participles.

1. The (excite) ______ fans cheered their team.
2. The fans enjoyed a really (excite) ______ game.
3. The (jump) ______ dolphins are the stars of the show.
4. The police found the (steal) ______ paintings in his car.
5. The prince kissed the (sleep) ______ princess.
6. Leonardo da Vinci designed a (fly) ______ machine.
7. We found a (hide) ______ door in the library.
8. The author tells us a (fascinate) ______ story.
9. The author read his story to a (fascinate) ______ audience.
10. The detective picked up a (use) ______ match.
11. The bridegroom[1] wore a (borrow) ______ suit.
12. I hate the sight of his (grin) ______ face!
13. Sandra is a very (love) ______ mother.
14. I dived into the (freeze) ______ water.
15. (Freeze) ______ food is popular with many families.

[1] Bräutigam

REMEMBER *Participle instead of a relative clause*

Partizipien kann man anstelle eines Relativsatzes benutzen. Die durchgestrichenen Wörter der Beispielsätze werden durch ein Partizip ersetzt:

Beispiele:

Alice is the woman ~~who is~~ serving the food. → Alice is the woman **serving** the food.
A clone is a copy of a person or animal ~~that~~ is grown in a laboratory. → A clone is a copy of a person or animal **grown** in a laboratory.

2 Complete the text with the correct participles.

1. The bank (hold up) ____ by gangsters offered a (tempt) ____ reward.
2. Many of the calls (make) ____ to the police were false, but one tip (send) ____ to the police as an e-mail led them to an (isolate) ____ farmhouse in Kent.
3. A team of forensic experts (search) ____ the farmhouse found important evidence.
4. They found the guns (use) ____ in the (frighten) ____ hold-up.
5. They also discovered in a washing machine the clothes (wear) ____ by the robbers.
6. Some banknotes (find) ____ on the kitchen floor came from the money (steal) ____ from the bank.
7. The van (report) ____ as parked outside the bank was in a garage.
8. The three (mask) ____ men (see) ____ in the car weren't in the farmhouse, but three passports (hide) ____ under a mattress belonged to them.
9. The passport photos (send) ____ online to all police stations in the country brought fast results: just two hours later, three men (stop) ____ by police on the M2 motorway were identified as the gangsters.
10. The robbers, (dress) ____ as hikers, were arrested.
11. The money (take) ____ from the bank was in two large rucksacks.

REMEMBER *Participle after a conjunction*

Nach einem Bindewort (Konjunktion) kann ein Partizip benutzt werden.
Achtung: Partizip (oder partizipialer Nebensatz) und Hauptsatz müssen dasselbe Subjekt haben.
Beispiele:
I often listen to the radio **while driving.**
Although stopped by the police, they were able to escape.
Cooks should always wash their hands **before handling** food.

3 Rewrite these sentences using a conjunction + participle.
Sometimes you must change other words, too.

EXAMPLE

All journeys are easy. You take one step at a time. → when
When taken one step at a time, all journeys are easy. Or:
All journeys are easy when taken one step at a time.

1. We went to bed. We turned the heating down. → Before
2. You use a grinder[1]. You should wear safety glasses. → When
3. The skier was buried under three metres of snow. He was found by the rescue dog. → Although
4. You take it too often. This drug can be harmful. → If
5. I always examine a car carefully. I buy it. → before
6. I always check my car's tyres. I start a long journey. → Before
7. The President was defeated in the election. He refused to go. → Although
8. You ask politely. Most people are helpful. → If

[1] Schleifmaschine

REMEMBER *Participles in sub-clauses*

Partizipien können benutzt werden in:

- Nebensätzen der Zeit,
- Nebensätzen des Grundes,
- Nebensätzen, die eine Reihe von Tätigkeiten beschreiben,
- Nebensätzen, die zusätzliche Informationen anbieten.

Achtung: Partizip (bzw. partizipialer Nebensatz) und Hauptsatz müssen dasselbe Subjekt haben.

Beispiele:
Having heard her sing before, I didn't want to repeat the experience.
Examining the room carefully, she found the hidden safe.
Watching him leave the house, I made a note of the time.
My friends told me about their fantastic holiday, **showing me lots of photos**.

4 Complete the sentences with the correct participial form.

1. (see) ______ the police fighting with football hooligans, the reporter stopped his car.
2. (grab) ______ his camera, he jumped out of his car.
3. (run) ______ towards the fighting, he took lots of photos.
4. (stand) ______ behind a phone box, he put a new film in his camera.
5. (notice/pick up) ______ a man ______ a brick, he moved closer.
6. (shout/throw) ______ loudly and ______ the brick, the man attacked a police officer.
7. (look/see) ______ through his camera and ______ the brick hit the policeman, the reporter took a series of photos.
8. (hold) ______ his head, the police officer fell to the ground.
9. (laugh/cheer) ______ and ______ the mob threw stones and bottles.
10. (notice/point at) ______ the reporter and ______ him, they ran after him.

1.9 *Articles and nouns*

REMEMBER *Indefinite and definite article*

Der unbestimmte Artikel *(indefinite article)* ist:
- **a** vor Konsonantenlauten und
- **an** vor Vokallauten.

Der unbestimmte Artikel kann nur in Verbindung mit zählbaren Substantiven *(countable nouns)* im Singular benutzt werden.
Beispiele: **an** apple, **a** plum, **a** pair of shoes

Der bestimmte Artikel *(definite article)* **the** bleibt gleich, wird aber unterschiedlich ausgesprochen.
Beispiele:

a uniform*	**the** [ðə] **u**nion*
an Australian	**the** [ði] **o**nion

(* Ausgesprochen wie 'youniform' und 'younion')

1 Insert the missing indefinite articles.

1. ___ European coin
2. ___ Italian ice cream
3. ___ university
4. ___ eel
5. ___ umbrella
6. ___ honorary member
7. ___ unpaid helper
8. ___ US state
9. ___ audience
10. ___ hour
11. ___ hourly message
12. ___ ukulele
13. ___ UN soldier
14. ___ unit
15. ___ universal truth
16. ___ universe
17. ___ Utopian philosophy
18. ___ aura
19. ___ honourable businessman
20. ___ UFO

REMEMBER *Indefinite article with occupation and religion*

Anders als im Deutschen wird a/an für Berufe und Glaubensrichtungen benutzt.
Beispiele:
My sister is **an** artist.
She was **a** Catholic, but now she's **an** atheist.

2 Insert the correct article where necessary.
(If nothing is needed, put an 'X'.)

Mr Gupta is ___ shopkeeper. Mr and Mrs Gupta are ___ Asians. They run ___ general store. It's ___ one at the corner of ___ street where Mr Whittaker lives. Mr Whittaker often goes for ___ early morning walk on Saturdays. He has ___ son who lives in ___ army camp in Germany. ___ large part of ___ British army is in ___ Germany. ___ Whittakers only have ___ one daughter. She's ___ waitress in ___ restaurant in Inverness, ___ port in ___ north of Scotland. ___ Taylors are ___ old couple. They're neighbours of ___ Whittakers. They're ___ people who live next door. They're all ___ pensioners.

REMEMBER *Articles with proper nouns*

Eigennamen *(proper nouns)* werden ohne Artikel gebraucht, es sei denn der Artikel ist ein Teil des Namens.
Beispiele:
We met John and Simon outside Harrod's in Oxford Street.
They live in the Bronx.
Hawaii is part of the United States of America.

Beachte die Bedeutungsunterschiede mit und ohne Artikel.
Beispiele:
I met Mr Hall. = Ich traf Herrn Hall.
I met **a** Mr Hall. = Ich begegnete einem gewissen Herrn Hall.
We met on Sunday. = Wir trafen uns am Sonntag.
We met on **a** Sunday. = Wir trafen uns an einem Sonntag.
We met in London. = Wir trafen uns in London.
We met in **a** London shrouded by fog. = Wir trafen uns in einem nebelverhüllten London (Schriftsprache – literarisch).
We'll meet again on **the** Sunday after Easter. = Wir treffen uns am Sonntag nach Ostern wieder.

3 Insert the correct article where necessary. (If nothing is needed, put an 'X'.)

I last saw ____ Tom Nash in ____ June. We were both in ____ New York. I think it was ____ Thursday, but I'm not sure. I remember that it was ____ week after ____ Thanksgiving. We had lunch together in ____ Fred's Diner. It's ____ nice traditional little restaurant opposite ____ Macy's on ____ Fifth Avenue. Towards ____ end of the meal ____ Mr Piper came to our table and spoke very quietly to ____ Tom. Tom told me that he had to leave with ____ Mr Piper and that they had to meet ____ Bill Grimes in ____ Central Park. Tom said he would meet me ____ hour later in ____ waiting room at ____ Grand Central Station. But I never saw either him or ____ Mr Piper again.

REMEMBER *Uncountable nouns*

Nicht zählbare Substantive *(uncountable nouns)* haben nur eine Einzahlform.
Beispiele:
The **bread is** fresh.
The **news is** good.
The **information was** useful.

Mit bestimmten Wendungen kann man Einzahl- und Mehrzahlformen bilden.
Beispiele:

a loaf of bread	→	two loaves of bread
an item of news	→	two items of news
a piece of information	→	two pieces of information

4 **Which of the following expressions can be used with these uncountable nouns? (Usually more than one is possible.)**

bar *slice* *strip* *jar* *can* *carton* *packet*
pound *piece* *bottle* *barrel* *jug* *litre*

1. a ______	of cheese	5. a ______	of milk
2. a ______	of bacon	6. a ______	of butter
3. a ______	of jam	7. a ______	of cake
4. a ______	of beer	8. a ______	of chocolate

GOOG TO KNOW *Animal collective nouns*

Bei Tieren werden bestimmte Sammelbegriffe benutzt.

Beispiele:

a herd of cows a flock of sheep a pride of lions a pack of wolves

5 **Name the animals and link the collective nouns with the animals.**

1. shoal/school	A	
2. flock/flight	B	
3. colony/army	C	
4. troop	D	
5. swarm	E	
6. cloud	F	
7. pride	G	
8. pod/school	H	
9. litter	I	
10. pack	J	

REMEMBER *Nouns with different singular and plural meanings*

Einige Substantive können unterschiedliche Bedeutungen haben – je nachdem, ob sie in der Einzahl oder Mehrzahl stehen.
Beispiele:
stair (Stufe) – stairs (Treppe) chocolate (Schokolade) – chocolates (Pralinen)

6 Link the English nouns with their German meanings.

1. glass	A Schmerz
2. glasses	B Stoff, Tuch
3. compass	C Brauch
4. compass(es)	D Brille *(formell)*
5. cloth	E Kompass
6. clothes	F Art, Weise
7. pain	G Manieren, Benehmen
8. pains	H Schauspiel
9. custom	J Glas
10. customs	K Mühe, Bemühung
11. manner	L Kleider, Kleidung
12. manners	M Brille *(ugs.)*
13. spectacle	N Zoll
14. spectacles	O Zirkel

REMEMBER *Plural nouns and pair nouns*

Es gibt eine kleine Gruppe von englischen Substantiven, die nur im Plural benutzt werden. Sie haben keine Einzahlformen. Vergleiche die englischen Sätze mit den deutschen Übersetzungen.
Beispiele:

The police **are** looking for me.	Die Polizei sucht nach mir.
The poor **are** always with us.	Die Armen sind immer unter uns.

Paarwörter *(pair words)* haben auch nur eine Mehrzahlform. Um eine Einzahlform zu bilden, benutzt man die Wendung a pair of.
Beispiele:

These scissors **are** blunt.	Diese Schere ist stumpf.
I've got **a pair of scissors**.	Ich habe eine Schere.
Your trousers **are** dirty.	Deine Hose ist schmutzig.
I need a new **pair of trousers**.	Ich brauche eine neue Hose.

Test

1 Infinitive (with or without *to*) or *ing*-form?

Complete the sentences with the correct form of the verbs in brackets. Sometimes two forms are possible.

1. Tom felt the huge hairy spider (crawl) ______ over his hand.
2. I'll show you where (buy) ______ the best fruit and vegetables in town.
3. It doesn't look good. You might (need) ______ your umbrella today.
4. I stopped because I needed (check) ______ the oil in the car.
5. Sandra likes (dance) ______ but she prefers modern dances.
6. We stood at the top of the cliffs and watched the sun (go) ______ down.
7. The policewoman persuaded the man (give) ______ her the gun.
8. Do you all know what (do) ______ in an emergency?
9. Susan ran over to the girl and helped her (get up) ______ .
10. We noticed a small dog (bury) ______ something in the garden.
11. I don't know how (get) ______ to the shopping centre from here.
12. I mustn't (get up) ______ ; the doctor told me (stay) ______ in bed.
13. I'd like (go) ______ fishing but I hate (get up) ______ early.
14. Doctor, I think you'd better (examine) ______ this patient again.
15. It's important for fishermen (listen to) ______ the weather forecast.
16. We think you should (stop) ______ the car (check) ______ the tyres.
17. I wrote an e-mail to Aunt Helen (tell) ______ her about the wedding.
18. Lots of people like (sing) ______ in the shower.
19. The new building will make it more difficult for the rats (get) ______ inside.
20. Who was the first person (swim) ______ the English Channel?
21. Caroline listened to her younger sister (play) ______ the piano.
22. Ricky loves science fiction and he can't wait (see) ______ the latest SF film.
23. I am not sure whether we can afford (buy) ______ a new car this year.
24. Whenever we go out he always forgets (take) ______ his keys.
25. I don't remember (buy) ______ that book, but I must have done so.
26. The firefighters left after the house had stopped (burn) ______ .
27. Nobody can force me (apologise) ______ for something I haven't done!
28. The purpose of the space station is (serve) ______ as a base for future exploration.

You get 1 point for each correct answer. **Your points:** ______ /31

2 Rewrite the sentences using participles.

1. After we had finished our meal, we drank some coffee.
2. Mrs Quinn is the woman who is selling tickets near the door.
3. The men who had been caught by the police were the thieves.
4. After I had watched the film, I took the dog for a walk.
5. Is this the football that was used in the World Cup?
6. Because we were very tired we went to bed at nine o'clock.
7. While I was walking home I had an accident.
8. After we had eaten a big meal we felt much better.
9. As soon as we saw the fire we called the fire brigade.
10. So this is the famous painting that was stolen from the museum.
11. As I watched the tiger I carefully took a photo.
12. When she looked out of the window she saw three men standing at the gate.
13. Any idiot can do it if they are correctly trained.
14. When you give people everything they want, they have nothing to work for.
15. If you stew it slowly in red wine, even tough meat will taste wonderful.

You get 1 point for each correct answer. **Your points:** ___ /15

3 Singular or plural? Underline the correct form of the verb.

1. Mr Westlake's manners was/were always perfect.
2. American cheese is/are usually very bland.
3. British food does/doesn't have a good reputation.
4. Some British foods is/are very popular in other countries.
5. The police is/are usually very helpful.
6. The new furniture goes/go in the dining room.
7. My new trousers is/are too short.
8. My new glasses is/are going to be very expensive.
9. Is/Are the scissors sharp?
10. Good advice is/are rare.

You get 1 point for each correct answer. **Your points:** ___ /10

Your total points out of 56: ___

- More than 47? Very good.
- More than 34? Good.
- Less than 28? Have a look at the grammar pages again.
  You CAN do better.

1.10 *Conjunctions and prepositions*

REMEMBER *Coordinating conjunctions*

Konjunktionen (Bindewörter) verbinden einzelne Wörter, Wendungen, Satzteile oder Sätze miteinander.

Koordinierende/nebenordnende Konjunktionen ***(coordinating conjunctions)*** verbinden Wörter oder Satzteile. Sie können auch Hauptsätze thematisch verbinden. Bei einer längeren Aufzählung werden Kommas gesetzt.

Beispiele:

Would you like beer **or** wine? **Or** would you prefer a soft drink?

We had fish **and** chips **and** two milkshakes, **and** then we had ice cream.

We had a picnic with ham **and** tomato sandwiches, cheese and crackers**, and** strawberries **and** cream.

1 Link these English conjunctions with their German meanings.

1.	and	A	nicht nur ... sondern auch
2.	or	B	sowohl ... als auch
3.	but	C	und auch; ebenso wie
4.	both ... and	D	weder ... noch
5.	not only ... but also	E	und
6.	either ... or	F	aber; sondern
7.	neither ... nor	G	oder
8.	as well as	H	entweder ... oder

REMEMBER *Subordinating conjunctions*

Subordinierende/unterordnende Konjunktionen stehen am Anfang eines Nebensatzes und verknüpfen ihn mit dem Hauptsatz.

Die häufigsten sind:

after, although/though, as, as soon as, as if, because, before, even if, if, (in order) to, since, so (that), that, (not) until, unless, when, whenever, whether, while.

Beispiele:

He often visits me **when** he has time.

Whenever you feel lonely, give me call.

As soon as I saw her face, I knew **that** something was wrong.

Beachte den Unterschied zwischen because (= weil) und because of (= wegen).
Beispiele:
I can't drive **because** I haven't got a driving licence.
We had to drive very slowly **because of** the thick fog.

2 Complete the sentences with suitable conjunctions.

because *that* *after/because* *so that* *but* *before* *Although*

1. His qualifications are good, ______ it was a long time ______ he found a job.
2. ______ his qualifications are good, it took him a long time to find a job.
3. The club changed the rules ______ they were unfair.
4. The club changed the rules ______ many people had complained ______ they were unfair.
5. The club changed the rules ______ men could join.

REMEMBER *And so/and neither (nor)*

Diese Konjunktionen werden als Zustimmungen in bejahenden bzw. verneinenden Sätzen benutzt.
Beispiele:
I liked the book, **and so** did my friends.
I don't have a chance, **and neither** (nor) do you.

3 Rewrite these sentences with the connectors *and so/and neither (nor).*

EXAMPLE

Jenny will just laugh at you. Her friends will laugh at you, too.
Jenny will just laugh at you, and so will her friends.

1. Mr Smith has got a bad temper. His wife has got a bad temper.
2. I'm frightened of dogs. My sister is also frightened of dogs.
3. I can't stand rap music. My friends can't stand it.
4. Jane hates science-fiction stories. Me, too.
5. Andy doesn't like Jeremy Warton. I don't like Jeremy Warton.
6. Mr Digby never smiles. His wife doesn't either.
7. Sunderland will never beat Manchester United. Middlesborough won't ever beat them either.

4 **Put in the missing connectors.**

after · *As/Because* · *as well as* · *because/as* · *because of* · *Both* · *and* · *but* · *even if* · *unless*

1. Tom ______ Mary often arrive at the sports club together. 2. ______ he ______ Mary work for the same firm, ______ not in the same department. 3. They're friends ______ colleagues. 4. ______ they also live near each other, they often share a car. 5. They usually go for a drink ______ leaving the sports club. 6. They always stop at the Jolly Sailors, ______ it's on their way home. 7. They like that pub ______ its friendly atmosphere. 8. Mary likes a gin and tonic ______ she's driving. 9. Tom never drinks alcohol ______ Mary is driving.

REMEMBER *Prepositions: in, on, at*

Diese drei Präpositionen werden im Englischen am häufigsten benutzt. Sie können sowohl als Orts- als auch als Zeitpräpositionen benutzt werden.

Beispiele:

Place	**Time**
Our meal is **in** the oven.	It'll be cooked **in** an hour or so.
The invitation is **on** the table.	The party is **on** March the tenth.
My parents are **at** work.	They'll be home **at** 5.30 p.m.

5 **Complete the sentences with *in*, *on* or *at*.**

Maria's birthday is ______ March. But it fell ______ a Friday this year, so her party was ______ the Saturday ______ her parents' house ______ Fox Terrace. Jack phoned me ______ the afternoon. He wanted me to wait for him ______ home, but I told him I'd be ______ the supermarket ______ Redcar Road. I thought about meeting him ______ the car park, but it's always full ______ Saturdays. So I asked him to meet me ______ the corner of Redcar Road and Church Lane ______ 7.30.

REMEMBER *More prepositions of time*

Weitere Präpositionen der Zeit sind:

after	(nach)	for	(seit: bei einem Zeitraum)
ago	(vor dem jetzigen Zeitpunkt)	from ... to	(von ... bis)
before	(vor)	since	(seit: bei einem Zeitpunkt)
between	(zwischen)	towards	(gegen)
by	(bis spätestens)	till/until	(bis)
during	(während)	not till/not until	(erst um/nicht vor)

Merke dir auch diese Präpositionen bei Uhrzeiten:
It was ten (minutes) **past** two. (BE: ... nach zwei Uhr)
It was ten minutes **after** two. (AE: ... nach zwei Uhr)
It was twenty-two minutes **to** two. (BE: ... vor zwei Uhr)
It was twenty-two minutes **before** two. (AE: ... vor zwei Uhr)

6 Complete the sentences with a suitable preposition of time.

after *for* *before* *till/until* *by* *during* *till/until* *since* *from ... till*

1. We went straight home ______ the match. (nach)
2. I went to the bank ______ my lunch break. (während)
3. I've been playing tennis ______ twenty years. (seit)
4. The garage will have our car ready ______ Tuesday afternoon. (bis)
5. We've been here ______ 3.30 yesterday morning! (seit)
6. I always read a book ______ I go to sleep. (vor/bevor)
7. The park is open ______ April ______ September. (von ... bis)
8. Can you stay ______ Mr Bradley arrives? (bis)
9. The fun doesn't really start ______ midnight. (erst um)

REMEMBER *More prepositions of place*

Die häufigsten Ortspräpositionen im Englischen sind:

above	(über, oberhalb)	by	(an, neben)
against	(gegen, an)	in front of	(vor)
among	(unter, inmitten)	inside	(innerhalb)
around (round)	(um, herum)	near	(nah)
before	(vor)	near to	(nah an)
behind	(hinter)	opposite	(gegenüber)
below	(unter, unterhalb)	outside	(außerhalb)
beside	(neben)	over	(über)
between	(zwischen)	under	(unter)

7 Complete the sentences with a suitable preposition of place.

among *near* *behind* *against* *outside* *around* *over/above*

1. I noticed a ladder standing ________ the garage wall. (gegen)
2. Sally stood ________ the sheep. (mitten unter)
3. Barbara's flat was ________ a bus stop. (in der Nähe von)
4. We sat ________ the table and talked. (um ... herum)
5. What's the temperature like ________ the building? (draußen)
6. There's a very big car park ________ the station. (hinter)
7. We hung the picture ________ the bed. (über/oberhalb)

REMEMBER *Prepositions of movement and direction*

Die häufigsten Richtungspräpositionen sind:

across	(quer, über)	off	(weg von)
after	(hinter, hinterher)	onto	(auf)
along	(entlang)	out of	(aus)
around/round	(um, um ... herum)	past	(nach, hinter, an ... vorbei)
down	(runter, hinunter, entlang)	through	(durch, hindurch)
from	(von ... entfernt)	to	(zu, nach)
into	(in ... hinein)	towards	(in Richtung, auf ... zu)
		up	(nach oben, hinauf, herauf)

8 Translate the sentences with a suitable preposition of movement.

1. Ich ging über die Straße.
2. Ich lief dem Bus hinterher.
3. Ich ging die Straße entlang.
4. Ich ging durch den Park.
5. Ich sah aus dem Fenster.
6. Ich ging ihm entgegen.
7. Ich ging in sein Büro.
8. Ich ging an ihm vorbei.
9. Tom war wütend und ging weg.

9 Translate the prepositions underlined in these sentences.

1. Susan Cornwall writes novels about a pathologist.
2. We used the branch as a ladder.
3. That picture was painted by my grandmother.
4. We're open every day except Sunday.
5. Tell Mike that I've got something for him.
6. What would you like for lunch?
7. Sue bought the wrong newspaper. She got the Sun instead of the Mirror.
8. This is a photo of the camping site in Spain.
9. Dick looks like a clown in those silly clothes!
10. There were over twenty people in the queue for the bus.
11. George came with his new girlfriend, Sarah.
12. You mustn't travel on the bus without a ticket.

REMEMBER *Phrasal verbs*

Verben mit Präposition und/oder Adverb haben entweder eine geänderte oder sogar eine völlig andere Bedeutung als das Verb allein.

Beispiele:

carry	(tragen)	carry off	(wegtragen)
carry out	(ausführen)	carry on	(weitermachen/Theater machen)
look	(schauen)	look in	(vorbeischauen)
look after	(aufpassen auf)	look around	(sich umschauen)
look into	(näher untersuchen)	look up	(nachschlagen)

10 Fill in the missing words. Look up the verbs you don't know in an English-German dictionary.

1. grow	______	(aufwachsen)
2. cut	______	(fällen)
3. cut	______	(abschneiden)
4. cut	______	(ausschneiden)
5. agree	______	(zustimmen)
6. show	______	(angeben)
7. ask	______	(bitten um)
8. give	______	(aufgeben)
9. drop	______	(ausscheiden)
10. break	______	(einbrechen)
11. break	______	(ausbrechen)
12. give	______	(verschenken)
13. fall	______	(zurückbleiben)
14. fall	______	(umfallen)
15. climb	______	(heraufklettern)
16. get	______	(aussteigen)
17. cheer	______	(ermuntern)
18. get	______	(aufstehen)
19. blow	______	(sprengen)
20. set	______	(errichten)
21. fill	______	(ausfüllen)
22. hand	______	(verteilen)
23. aim	______	(zielen auf)
24. find	______	(herausfinden)

1.11 *Translating* wollen, sollen, lassen

REMEMBER wollen

Entscheidungen und Absichtserklärungen werden oft mit want to + Infinitiv übersetzt.
Beispiel:
Wir wollen gewinnen. = We want to win.

Bei Wünschen kannst du zwischen want to und would like to wählen.
Beispiel:
Wer will der Nächste sein? = Who wants to be next?/Who would like to be ...?

Achtung! Eine Aufforderung mit want (to) kann im Englischen in bestimmten Situationen als ziemlich ruppig empfunden werden - auch mit please. Überlege, welchen Eindruck du mit der Übersetzung machst:
Ich will Milch in meinem Kaffee, bitte.
- ruppig = I want milk in my coffee, please!
- höflich = I'd like milk in my coffee, please.

Weigerungen bzw. Ablehnungen können mit do not want to oder auch mit won't übersetzt werden. Die Übersetzung mit won't wirkt betont und entschlossener.
Beispiele:
Ich will nicht gehen. = I don't want to go./I won't go.
Sie wollen es mir nicht sagen. = They don't want to tell me./They won't tell me.
Er wollte nicht mit mir sprechen. = He didn't want to talk to me./He wouldn't ...

Wenn die Übersetzung eine formelle Situation wiedergeben soll, kann „wollen" mit wish to übersetzt werden.
Beispiele:
Der Spender will anonym bleiben. = The donor wishes to remain anonymous.
Maria und Sven wollen die Geburt ihrer Tochter Sophie bekanntgeben. = Maria and Sven wish to announce the birth of their daughter Sophie.

1 How would you translate *wollen* in these sentences?

1. Ich will Französisch lernen. = ______
2. Wollen Sie Mayonnaise auf Ihre Pommes Frites? = ______
3. Der Vorstand will allen Mitarbeitern gratulieren. = ______
4. Tom wollte nicht aufhören zu reden. = ______
5. Ich will deine Handynummer, bitte. = ______

REMEMBER sollen

„Sollen“ kann im Deutschen mehrere Bedeutungen haben. Es gibt im Englischen entsprechend viele Möglichkeiten, diese unterschiedlichen Aspekte zu übersetzen.

Beispiele:

▶ Ein Vorschlag:
(Es schmeckt gut.) Du solltest es probieren. = You **should/ought to** try it.
Sollen wir gehen? = **Shall/Should** we go?

▶ Ein Versprechen:
Unser neues EDV-Programm soll das Problem lösen. = Our new program **should/ought to** solve that problem./Our new program **is intended to** solve that problem. (recht formell)

▶ Ein Gerücht oder eine Behauptung wird meistens mit einer Passivform übersetzt:
Er soll sehr klug sein. = He **is supposed to be** very clever./He **is said to be** very clever./**I'm told** he's very clever.

▶ Eine Empfehlung oder eine Warnung (besonders beim Signalwort „lieber“):
(Der Chef kommt.) Ihr solltet lieber schnell gehen! = You'**d better** leave quickly!
Wir sollten die Polizei rufen! = We'**d better** call the police!

2 How would you translate *sollen* in these sentences?

1. Vielleicht sollte ich mehr  sparen. =
2. Wie sollen wir das Rätsel lösen? =
3. Soll ich hier auf dich warten? =
4. Diese  soll Wunder wirken. =
5. Die Schotten sollen ziemlich geizig sein. =
6. Sie sollten keine  sammeln, die Sie nicht kennen. =
7. Die Suppe ist versalzen. Sie sollten lieber etwas Sahne dazugeben. =
8. Sie sollten verschwinden und zwar sofort! =
9. Was soll es sein? =
10. Diese Maßnahmen sollen das Problem lösen. =
11. Mehr als 200 Beschäftigte sollen entlassen werden. =

REMEMBER lassen

Die unterschiedlichen Bedeutungen von „lassen“ müssen jeweils anders übersetzt werden.

Beispiele:

- Etwas veranlassen:
  Ich ließ die Hecke schneiden. = I **had** the hedge cut.
- Etwas erzwingen:
  Er ließ mich stundenlang warten. = He **made** me wait for hours.
- Mit etwas aufhören:
  Sie kann es nicht lassen! = She can't stop (doing) it!
- Etwas erlauben/zulassen:
  Lasst ihn nicht herein! = Don't let him (come) in!
- Etwas zurücklassen:
  Ich habe meinen Mantel im Auto gelassen. = I've left my coat in the car.
- Etwas ist möglich:
  Das lässt sich machen. = It can be done.
  Es lässt sich leicht reparieren. = It can be repaired easily.
  Die Richterin wird sich schwer überzeugen lassen. = The judge won't be easy to convince.

3 **Translate these sentences. Use a German-English dictionary for any words you don't know.**

1. Sie ließen das Auto stehen und gingen zu Fuß weiter.
2. Sie ließ ihn nicht mit ihrem Spielzeug spielen.
3. Er kann das Fluchen nicht lassen.
4. Einmal im Jahr lassen wir das Auto warten.
5. Ich ging hinein und ließ mir die Haare schneiden.
6. Sie ließen mich für die zerbrochene Vase zahlen.
7. Sie lässt uns nichts erklären.
8. Ich ließ die Hecke schneiden.
9. Er ließ uns stundenlang warten.
10. Lasst den Hund nicht herein.

Test

1 What are the plural forms?

1. thief
2. chimney
3. sheep
4. breadknife
5. forget-me-not
6. wolf
7. fish
8. chief
9. tooth
10. fisherman
11. shopping bag
12. fly

You get 1 point for each correct answer. Your points: /12

2 What are these nouns: proper nouns (P), countable nouns (C), or uncountable nouns (U)?

1. air
2. Adam
3. chalk
4. policeman
5. milk
6. rabbit
7. Italy
8. furniture
9. box
10. tea
11. shark
12. battleship
13. mouse
14. butter
15. York

You get 1 point for each correct answer. Your points: /15

3 Collectives/singulars/plurals: write the English equivalents.

1. ein Laib Brot
2. eine Hose
3. der Zoll
4. Benehmen
5. eine Schere
6. ein Zirkel
7. eine Nachricht
8. ein Fass Bier
9. eine Tafel Schokolade
10. eine Schachtel Pralinen

You get 1 point for each correct answer. Your points: /10

4 Translate these sentences.

1. Meine Mutter ist Ärztin.
2. Sie arbeitet im Krankenhaus in der Victoria Road.
3. Mein Vater ist Verkäufer.
4. Er arbeitet im Asco-Supermarkt in der Cromwell Street.

You get 2 points for each correct sentence. **Your points:** ____ /8

5 Complete the sentences with the conjunctions/connectors.

after *although* *and* *and neither* *and so* *as* *as soon as*
because *because of* *before* *but* *if* *or* *since*
unless *until* *until* *when* *when* *Whenever*
whenever *while*

1. We had hardly finished our meal ______ the phone started ringing.
2. We couldn't ask questions ______ the end of her talk.
3. The waiter wasn't only lazy, ______ rude, too.
4. Which would you prefer: a beef steak ______ a pork pie?
5. In England, fish ______ chips always go together.
6. I didn't eat it ______ it smelled bad.
7. Many people won't eat garlic ______ its smell.
8. I give her money ______ I can.
9. Don't try the roller coaster ______ it frightens you.
10. Don't take part in the marathon ______ you have trained hard.
11. My parents didn't enjoy it, ______ did I.
12. Mandy was born in South Africa, ______ was her brother.
13. It started to rain just ______ we were coming out of the cinema.
14. You mustn't go swimming immediately ______ eating a big meal.
15. ______ I hear that tune I think of my schooldays. We used to sing it in assembly.
16. This letter is very urgent. I want you to answer it ______ you can.
17. I'll wait here ______ you come.
18. ______ you answer any of these questions you should revise the grammar section.
19. Ann did the crossword ______ Pete was cooking the dinner.
20. Could you get me a newspaper ______ you go past the station please?
21. I have not seen John ______ he went to live in Edinburgh.
22. I think we should give him a second chance, ______ he doesn't really deserve it.

You get 1 point for each correct answer. **Your points:** ____ /22

6 Fill in the missing prepositions.

1. I went straight home ______ the concert. (nach)
2. Bill went to sleep ______ the film. (während)
3. We've lived here ______ twenty-five years. (seit)
4. Jim has lived in New York ______ 1999. (seit)
5. We had to wait ______ the post office opened. (bis)
6. Jennifer was standing ______ two paintings. (zwischen)

You get 1 point for each correct answer. Your points: ___ /6

7 What are the most suitable opposites?

1. after ______
2. below. ______
3. behind ______
4. up ______
5. inside ______
6. under ______
7. with ______
8. out of ______

You get 1 point for each correct answer. Your points: ___ /8

8 What are the missing words in these phrasal verbs?

1. weitermachen: carry ______
2. verschenken: give ______
3. ausführen: carry ______
4. verzichten auf: give ______

You get 1 point for each correct answer. Your points: ___ /4

9 Translate these sentences into English. Use *may, shall, ought to.*

1. Dürfen wir jetzt gehen?
2. Ich habe ihn vielleicht gekannt.
3. Soll ich ein Fenster aufmachen?
4. Er sollte sich schämen.
5. Darf ich mich hier hinsetzen?
6. Das mag sein, aber es ist trotzdem falsch.
7. Sie mögen Recht haben.
8. Du solltest mit deinen Eltern darüber reden.

You get 2 points for each correct sentence. Your points: ___ /16

10 **Translate these words into German and write the German words in the crossword puzzle.**

Across 4. spectacle 6. cloth 8. customs 9. scissors 12. police 13. tweezers 14. cattle 15. clothes

Down 1. pains 2. pain 3. glasses 4. sheep 5. salmon 7. manners 10. trousers 11. pliers

You get 1 point for each correct word. **Your points:** ____ /16

Your total points out of 117: ____

- More than 99? Very good.
- More than 87? Good.
- Less than 58? Have a look at the grammar pages again.
  You CAN do better.

2 Texte verstehen

Das solltest du am Ende der Klasse 10 können:

im Bereich Lesen und verstehen:

- ▷ Selbstständig umfangreichere authentische (d. h. nicht für Schulbücher geschriebene) Texte verstehen und dabei sowohl die Informationen aus dem Text als auch allgemeines Weltwissen zum Verständnis heranziehen
- ▷ Sachtexten wesentliche Punkte entnehmen und Einzelinformationen in den Gesamtzusammenhang einordnen
- ▷ Texte sowohl global als auch im Detail verstehen
- ▷ Inhaltlich wichtige Passagen identifizieren und in Notizen festhalten

im Bereich Hören und verstehen:

- ▷ Deutlich gesprochenen Berichten in Rundfunk und Fernsehen zu vertrauten Themen sowie klar strukturierten Internet-Angeboten wichtige Informationen entnehmen
- ▷ Das Wesentliche aus deutlich artikulierten Liedern verstehen
- ▷ Vorbereitete Telefonate führen
- ▷ Nachrichten notieren, wenn jemand nach Informationen fragt oder ein Problem erläutert
- ▷ Hörtexte sowohl global als auch im Detail verstehen

2.1 Lesen und verstehen

GOOD TO KNOW | **Unbekannte Wörter**

Um die unbekannten Wörter eines Textes zu verstehen, musst du nicht in jedem Fall im Wörterbuch nachschlagen. Das ist lästig und verdirbt den Spaß am Lesen. Die gängigen Strategien, Bedeutungen zu erschließen, sollten dir geläufig sein:

- ▶ **Wortfamilien**
  Häufig kennst du bereits ein Wort, das mit dem unbekannten Wort verwandt ist. Beispiel: Das Wort apologetically in Z. 18 des folgenden Textes von Beini Shi ist verwandt mit dem Wort apologise, das du schon lange kennst. Außerdem weißt du, dass -ic häufig eine Adjektivendung ist, somit sollte die Bedeutung „entschuldigend" klar werden.

- ▶ **Ähnlichkeiten mit Wörtern anderer Sprachen**
  Neben Englisch kennst du andere Sprachen, v. a. Deutsch, womöglich aber auch Französisch, Spanisch oder andere Sprachen. Viele Wörter sind sich in den

europäischen Sprachen ähnlich, sodass du sie leicht erkennen kannst. Ein Beispiel aus dem Text wäre to ignore (Z. 20).

- **Kontext**
  Die wichtigste Strategie, Wörter und Wortgruppen zu verstehen, ist, den Kontext – also den thematischen Zusammenhang – zu begreifen. Selbst wenn man die exakte Bedeutung nicht versteht, so gibt der Kontext doch zumindest Aufschluss über die ungefähre Bedeutung eines Wortes. Was bedeutet z. B. assigned in Z. 12? Wir wissen, dass es um Schule und ein „project" geht. Das Verb wird also benutzt in Zusammenhang mit Aufgaben, die Schüler bekommen. Es bedeutet also „aufgeben" oder „zuweisen".

- **Klang**
  Oft verrät einfach der Klang eines Wortes etwas über seine Bedeutung. Ein Beispiel aus dem Text ist to mumble, dt. „murmeln" (Z. 16).

Not Asian Enough

Track 2

1 **What strategy would you use to understand the following words from the text?**

Put the words in a table (see below). Sometimes the same word can be put in more than one column.

fluently *aroma* *sticky* *dessert* *frown*
disrespectful *pretend* *facial* *spit out*

word family	similarity to German	context
sticky	...	...
...		

2 Read the following text.

"Not Asian enough" is an article from the American online youth magazine *LA Youth*.
After reading, do the following tasks. Sometimes you have to write the answer. In other tasks you have to choose the correct answer from several options.
You can also listen to the text on the CD.

Not Asian Enough

By Beini Shi

My life started out as a typically Asian story. I was five when my mom decided to move from China to the United States to give me better opportunities. I started school a few days after we arrived in Salt Lake City, Utah, and I was the shy Chinese girl whose only English words were "yes" and "no." I was one of just two Asian people in my class. But after just a few months I could speak English almost fluently and my mom was reminding me to speak more Mandarin at home. [...]

It was once we moved to Los Angeles in 1996 that my story changed. No longer was I the new, quiet Chinese girl who couldn't say more than a sentence in English. Now I was the new Chinese girl who turned out to be not Asian enough for some of her Asian classmates.

For the first time, I was around a lot of Asian people at school. In seventh grade we were assigned a project to make dinner for our families. I went over to my friend's house to make the meal. We didn't end up doing much of the cooking (my friend's mom did most of it). When the meal was finished, its aroma spread throughout her house – wontons, egg rolls, beef and a sticky rice cake for dessert. When we sat down at the table I was hungry, so I put a piece of beef in my mouth. My friend's father frowned at me and mumbled under his breath in Chinese, "How rude and disrespectful."

I was confused. Obviously I wasn't going to spit the meat out, so I just smiled apologetically, and he didn't say any more. He didn't look too happy, though. I wasn't sure what to do, so I decided to ignore his facial expression and continued eating. Then everyone just dug in and pretended as if nothing had happened.

I told my mom what happened later. She explained to me that my friend's family must follow the Chinese tradition in which the father eats first at dinner, then the mother, then the children, in order of age. I was embarrassed that I didn't know this tradition, but it wasn't my fault. No one had ever told me about it. My mom said that her family sometimes followed this when they lived in China. I asked a few of my other Asian friends about it and they were surprised I didn't know. Most of them told me that it was "an unsaid type of thing." It didn't matter all that much, but it was respectful if you did it. Not all of their families were strict about it.

It occurred to me that there were some really traditional Asian families out there. [...]

I liked that my mother was open to a more American lifestyle. I felt that my friend and her family didn't think I was Asian enough, while I thought they were a little out of touch with the times. [...]

GOOD TO KNOW **Multiple-Choice-Aufgaben**

Bei Multiple-Choice-Aufgaben ist es wichtig, dass man nicht nur auf Schlüsselwörter schaut, die eine vermeintlich richtige Lösung nahelegen. Oft ist das ein Trick, der dazu dient, zu genauem Lesen anzuhalten.

3 **Complete the sentences or choose the correct answer.**

1. The article is about ...
   a. cultural differences.
   b. mixed-race families.
   c. racism.
   d. traditional cooking.

2. Why did Beini Shi and her mother move to America?
   Because ...

3. When she arrived in Salt Lake City, Beini Shi ...
   a. was in a class with a lot of white pupils.
   b. spoke fluent English after a few days.
   c. could not even say "yes" or "no" in English.
   d. was reminded by her mom to eat more fruit.

4. In Los Angeles, Beini Shi ...
   a. did not have enough Asian classmates.
   b. was a quiet girl.
   c. had no white classmates.
   d. was different from her Asian classmates.

5. At school ...
   a. they did a food project.
   b. they made a 7-course dinner.
   c. they signed on for school dinner.
   d. they brought their families in for dinner.

6. When having dinner with her friend's family, Beini Shi ...
   a. did not like the food and had to spit it out.
   b. did not pay proper respect to her friend's parents.
   c. did not want to eat Chinese food.
   d. was confused about the different types of food.

7. How did her friend's father feel about Shi's behaviour?

8. What is the traditionally correct order for a Chinese family to start a meal?
   Put the following family members in the correct order:
   daughter (10 years), mother (41 years), father (39 years), son (7 years)

9. This order ...
   a. does not matter at all to Asians.
   b. must never be talked about in Asian families.
   c. is a widely accepted tradition.
   d. is a strict rule.

10. Beini Shi ...
    a. did not care about Chinese traditions.
    b. felt bad because she had not behaved correctly.
    c. wanted to learn about Chinese traditions.
    d. was angry because she didn't know these traditions.

11. Did Beini Shi prefer an American way of life to an Asian way of life?
    Yes: she writes ...
    No: she writes ...

12. Beini Shi thought some of her Asian classmates were ...
    a. cool.
    b. old-fashioned.
    c. untouchable.
    d. up to date.

Failing Teachers

Track 3

Im folgenden Text kommt zum Leseverstehen das ***note taking*** hinzu. In verschiedenen Teilaufgaben wirst du aufgefordert, wesentliche Inhaltspunkte stichwortartig zu benennen. Dies ist eine Technik, die du insbesondere beim Lesen schwieriger Texte anwenden solltest. Stichworte sind gewöhnlich Substantive, Adjektive, Verben oder Zahlen. Ganze Sätze halten zu sehr auf und sind unübersichtlich.

GOOD TO KNOW *Note taking* – Notizen machen

Wenn du mit Informationen, die du beim Lesen und Hören von Texten erhalten hast, in irgendeiner Form weiterarbeiten sollst (z. B. Aufgaben lösen, die Informationen bearbeiten und vortragen), ist es sinnvoll, Notizen zu machen.
Weil du oft wenig Zeit oder Raum hast, ist es hilfreich, wenn du ...

- nur die wichtigsten Informationen notierst (Schlüsselbegriffe, die sich oft aus der Aufgabenstellung ergeben),
- Abkürzungen oder Symbole – auch Zahlen – benutzt (stelle aber sicher, dass du diese auch später noch verstehst),
- eine tabellenförmige Vorstrukturierung anfertigst (insbesondere bei Prüfungsaufgaben wird dies vorgegeben sein).

1 **Apply the same strategies to *Failing Teachers* that you used for the previous text.**
What strategy would you use to understand the following words from the text?
Put the words in a table (see below). Sometimes the same word can be put in more than one column.

successful *destructive* *loathing* *noisy* *urban*
thug *require* *plague* *categorize* *undisciplined*
administrator *diligent*

word family	similarity to German	context
successful	...	...
...		

2 **Read the text.**

“Failing Teachers” is an article from the *New York Times*.
Read the article carefully. After reading it, do the following tasks. Sometimes you have to write the answer. In other tasks you have to choose the correct answer from several options.

You can also listen to the text on the CD.

Failing Teachers

By Bob Herbert, The New York Times, October 24, 2003

I’ve been talking recently with a handful of dedicated teachers about the classroom conditions that have prevailed over the past few years at some of New York City’s least successful high schools. These are places where fear and loathing take up the space that could have been occupied by progress and reform.
You’ll find these noisy, chaotic classrooms in almost any of America’s big cities, not just New York. They are extremely destructive, and scary to students and teachers alike. They are places where childhood dreams all too often end.
“Sisyphus[1], that’s me,” said one teacher. “But I won’t give up because I can’t bear to walk away from these kids.” [...]
“What goes on in these classrooms, that’s the story of urban education,” said a teacher from Brooklyn. “You’ve got kids playing dice in the back of the classroom. You’ve got kids listening to their Walkman, or writing rap rhymes. And rapping to girls. And also practicing gang signs. Now that’s a classroom that’s run by a teacher who doesn’t care.” [...]
“Remember,” said a teacher from Manhattan, “these are just children. Teenagers. There is no reason to ever let them get out of control like that. But I would say that many of the teachers I’ve met don’t care about their students.”
A male teacher who runs very disciplined classes in Brooklyn spoke of the fear that plagues teachers and students in some schools. “You have violence in some of our schools, and people react to violence in different ways,” he said. “You have teachers who have categorized all of the students as a problem. So they walk into the room afraid of the students without ever knowing them. To them, the students are one-dimensional. Everybody’s a thug. Everybody’s a problem. So they don’t require anything of any of them.”
“Meanwhile, the students themselves are scared. The class becomes undisciplined, and therefore dangerous. So the good students cut out because they don’t want to be in that environment. That’s one way you lose the good kids. You have a lot of students who are not thugs, but who left school because they couldn’t learn – they couldn’t even hear – in that noisy atmosphere.”

[1] Sisyphus, in Greek mythology, had to roll a stone up a hill, but as soon as he reached the top, the stone rolled down again.

The teachers I talked to spread the blame widely among students, parents, teachers and administrators. But they were hardest on teachers.
"You have teachers who are very diligent," said a middle-aged teacher from the Bronx. "They work very hard, and even come up with money out of their own pockets to pay for supplies, or even to help these children when they are in trouble. But there are many, many others who are not at all interested in these kids. They tell the kids to their faces: 'I don't care what you do. I'm still going to get paid.'" [...]

3 Complete the sentences or answer the questions.

1. Some New York high schools ...
   a. are frightening places for teachers and students.
   b. are undergoing progressive reform.
   c. are very successful.
   d. have bad air-conditioning in their classrooms.
2. Is this just a problem of New York City?
   Yes: the text says ...
   No: the text says ...
3. Who do the teachers hold responsible for the situation in New York schools?
4. What different kinds of behaviour do New York students show? Give several examples.
5. What makes a New York teacher feel like Sisyphus?
6. What is meant by "one-dimensional" students?
   a. Students are either good or bad.
   b. Students are interested in just one thing.
   c. Students are not particularly intelligent.
   d. Students are not seen as individuals.
7. What characterizes a good inner-city teacher? Make a list.
8. What is the main criticism of their colleagues that New York teachers express?
9. What happens to the good students?
10. Which alternative headline would match the article from the *New York Times* best?
    a. Crime rate rises in New York schools
    b. New York schools less successful than others
    c. Parents must look after their kids
    d. Schools – places of fear and indifference

2.2 Hören und verstehen

GOOD TO KNOW **Tipps zum globalen Hörverstehen**

Du musst nicht jedes Wort verstehen. Um allgemein zu verstehen, worum es geht, achte ...

- auf den **Kontext**. Allein deine Erwartung durch die Überschrift wird dir beim Verständnis helfen. So wirst du im folgenden Text Wörter wie cowboy, pioneer oder trapper eher verstehen, weil du sie in diesem Zusammenhang erwartest.
- auf **Schlüsselwörter**. Das allgemeine Verständnis wird nicht von einem einzelnen Wort abhängen, sondern vom Zusammenspiel einzelner Informationen, die auch häufig wiederholt werden.
- auf **Nebengeräusche**, die dir helfen, den Text einzuordnen, z. B. Autos oder Geschirrklappern.

The Museum of the American West — Track 4

You are visiting "The Museum of the American West" in a little town in Colorado. You have got an audio guide (headphones) that tells you about all the objects in the museum.

1 Listen to the texts and match them with the pictures.

Text 1	picture		Text 5	picture		Text 9	picture	
Text 2	picture		Text 6	picture		Text 10	picture	
Text 3	picture		Text 7	picture		Text 11	picture	
Text 4	picture		Text 8	picture				

E

F

G

GOOD TO KNOW **Tipps zum detaillierten Hörverstehen**

Bei manchen Hörverstehensaufgaben geht es eher um Einzelinformationen. Auch hier ist es nicht schlimm, wenn du nicht jedes Wort verstehst. Wichtige Informationen werden oft wiederholt.
Achte zusätzlich auf **Stimme** und **Betonung** der Sprecher. Wichtige Informationen werden sie anders betonen als unwichtige.
Mach dir während des Hörens nur kurze **Notizen** in Stichworten. Für ganze Sätze hast du keine Zeit.

The Lakeside Hotel

Track 5

You and your friend Brian are on holiday in the Lake District and have just arrived at your hotel. You want to get some information on your holidays from your tour guide. Because your friend is having a rest and you do not want to forget any important information, you have prepared a piece of paper with all the things you want to know. When the travel club representative welcomes all the new guests, you have your paper ready to fill in the information.

1 **First, look at the answer sheet below. Then listen to what the travel club representative says.**
Listen to the text twice.

2 **Now write the information in the appropriate spaces.**
Remember, you can fill in the gaps while you are listening.

1. **Contact** the travel club representative:
   In the hotel ______
   ______
   When he is not in the hotel: ______
2. **Meals:**
   Breakfast is from ______,
   it's ______ service in the ______ Lounge.
   Lunch: From ______
   in the ______.
   Dinner: From ______
   in the ______.
   Try the ______!
3. **Trips:** Can arrange boat trips, walking tours and ______ trips.
4. **Sports facilities** at the hotel:
   fitness centre, ______ room, sauna, ______.
   How much does it cost? ______
   Please remember: ______
5. **Friday Special:**
   What is this? ______ cruise with disco.
   How much does it cost? ______
   Where does the boat sail from? ______.
   When? From ______ to ______.
6. **Remember**
   You must take the tour guide's ______ with his mobile phone number.

Beamish North of England Open Air Museum

Track 6

Your class wants to visit the North of England Open Air Museum. Your teacher has asked you to get in touch with the museum and find out the latest information on a number of points. To make things easier for you, she has prepared a grid for you to fill in. You call the information line of the museum and hear the following announcement.

1 First, look at the grid below, then listen to the information line, then fill in the grid or tick (✔) the correct answer.
Listen to the text twice. And remember, you can fill in the grid while you are listening.

What you need to ask	Answers/information
Ticket prices for school groups	
- pupils	
- teachers	
Opening times	
Tuesday - Sunday	
Monday	
How to get there if there is a bus	
- where can you get on?	at ______ via Gateshead, ______ and Chester-le-Street
- how much is it?	
Food and drink	
- special advice/rules for schools	
Activities - is there an activity about	
- the life of a pupil 150 years ago?	yes / no
- cooking like your great-grandparents?	yes / no
- life on a farm?	yes / no
- the life of a fishwife?	yes / no
- railways?	yes / no
How much are the activities?	
When must you book the activities?	
Contact	
- web address	
- e-mail address	

Test

Sarah wants to be an au-pair

Track 7

Sarah wants to spend a year in England as an au-pair. She has found an advertisement in a newspaper offering a job as an au-pair in a family in London. Now she is phoning the number given in the ad. Listen to the telephone conversation and complete the statements below by filling the gaps or ticking the correct boxes.

1 First, look at the statements, then listen to the telephone conversation, then fill in the gaps or tick the correct boxes.
Listen to the text twice. And remember, you can write your solutions while you are listening. There is always only one correct answer.

1. Patrick's phone number is ______.
2. Sarah has read an ad in ______.
3. Patrick wants Sarah to start work in ______.
4. Sarah must look after ...
   a. all the members of the family.
   b. all the children in the Anderson family.
   c. the youngest members of the Anderson family.
5. Sarah must look after the twins ...
   a. before kindergarten and between kindergarten and dinner.
   b. from 8 a.m. to 7 p.m.
   c. only in the afternoon.
6. Sarah must help with shopping ...
   a. at the weekend.
   b. one day a week.
   c. one Saturday a month.

	true	false
7. Sarah must have a driving licence.	☐	☐
8. You can't get to Tracy and Linda's kindergarten by car.	☐	☐
9. Patrick is the only driver in the Anderson family.	☐	☐
10. The Anderson's house is only five years old.	☐	☐
11. Patrick works as a steel engineer.	☐	☐
12. Sarah will have her own bathroom.	☐	☐

13. The au-pair agency will look after Sarah's __________,
__________, and __________.

14. During her year in London, Sarah can go home at __________ and at
__________.

15. The Andersons will pay for Sarah's flights __________ of her stay,
__________ of her stay and for __________ visit home.

16. The Andersons' last au-pair went __________ at Christmas and
__________ at Easter.

17. Sarah wants to work from September to August because __________
__________.

18. Sarah's reference number with Au-Pair-World-Wide is __________

19. Sarah's e-mail address is __________.

20. Patrick's e-mail address is: __________.

You get 1 point for each correct answer. **Your points:** ____ /26

Your total points out of 26 points: ____

- More than 22? Very good.
- More than 19? Good.
- Less than 13? Have a look at the pages in this chapter again.
  You CAN do better.

3 Texte schreiben

Das solltest du am Ende der Klasse 10 können:

im Bereich literarische Texte:

- ▷ Inhaltliche und stilistische Besonderheiten von Texten und ihre Wirkung erkennen (u.a. Figurendarstellung, *setting, atmosphere,* Handlungsverlauf)
- ▷ Texten wesentliche Punkte entnehmen
- ▷ Kreativ schreiben
- ▷ Texte persönlich wertend kommentieren
- ▷ Argumentative Sachtexte schreiben
- ▷ Texte ausformen und umformen

im Bereich nicht-literarische Texte:

- ▷ Weitgehend selbstständig zusammenhängende Texte zu Themen deines Interessens- und Erfahrungsbereichs sowie zu Themen von gesellschaftlicher Bedeutung verfassen
- ▷ In beschreibender, berichtender, erzählender, zusammenfassender und argumentativer Form strukturiert schreiben
- ▷ Sachtexte bzw. literarische Texte bezogen auf Inhalt und Form persönlich wertend kommentieren
- ▷ Sachverhalte und Arbeitsergebnisse angemessen darstellen und erläutern
- ▷ Problemstellungen erörtern und dazu argumentierend Stellung nehmen

3.1 Über erzählende Texte *(fiction)* schreiben

REMEMBER Aufbau von Textaufgaben – erzählende Texte

Textaufgaben ähneln sich im Aufbau. Sie bestehen aus mehreren Teilaufgaben. Der erste Teil wird eine inhaltliche Frage sein. Es wird also eine **Inhaltsangabe** *(summary)* erwartet. Danach schließt sich logisch eine **Analyseaufgabe** *(analysis)* an. Hier geht es um die Gestaltung des Textes, die Gliederung, die Erzählweise oder Erzählperspektive, um Sprache, Metaphorik, Symbolik. Es kann auch um die Darstellung der Charaktere gehen oder um die Schaffung einer bestimmten Atmosphäre.
In der Regel schließt sich dann eine Teilaufgabe an, die über den Text hinausgeht. Das kann eine **persönliche Stellungnahme** *(comment)* sein – in diesem Band Teilaufgabe 3. a) – oder eine **kreative Schreibaufgabe** *(creative task)* – in diesem Band Teilaufgabe 3. b). Beides hat immer mit Wertung zu tun, denn auch für den kreativen Umgang mit der Textvorlage muss man die Problematik des Textes durchdrungen haben. Man kann z. B. keinen Perspektivwechsel vornehmen, wenn man nicht bereits einen Blinkwinkel verstanden hat.

Beispiel:

Für den folgenden Text „Can I Help You?" könnte die Aufgabenstellung so aussehen:

1. Describe the encounter of the narrator and her customer.
2. Describe what the narrator so strongly dislikes about the lady.
3. a) "Reason and compassion are qualities reserved for the working class." (line 29–30) Do you agree? Are poor people more reasonable than rich people? Are they more compassionate? Give arguments for and against the narrator's statement and draw your own conclusion.
   b) The assistant in the bookshop next door likes the lady and her behaviour. Write a short episode in which he/she describes the lady as she appears in the shop.

Im Folgenden kannst du nun diese Aufgaben Schritt für Schritt bearbeiten.

How to write about a text – character

1 Read the text carefully.
You can also listen to the text on the CD.

Can I Help You? — Track 8

By Sam B.

Her thin lips spread to reveal[1] white teeth, too white. Or maybe it's not that her teeth are too white, maybe it's the contrast created by the pink, diseased[2], old-lady gums that makes her smile seem unnatural. Her eyes don't help – they are far too squinty[3] and sparkling, and day-old mascara clings to the inside corners. She wears a crisp white pantsuit[4]. Expensive and appropriate[5]. She smells of perfume and old money. A printed silk shirt hangs loosely off her frail[6] shoulders. The baubles[7] on her spider-fingers tap against the glass bakery counter, a call to attention for my co-workers and me.
I stop stacking the bread shelf and turn to the counter where she stands, impatient. We make eye contact. Realizing my mistake, I shift my eyes and look pleadingly at Cassandra, my co-worker. She returns my gaze with a look that seems to say, you saw her first. You deal with her. James, the other cashier, is elbow-deep in dishes at the sink.

[1] to show; [2] looking ill; [3] partly closed; [4] Hosenanzug; [5] suitable; [6] thin and weak; [7] Tand

Sighing[8], I brush the breadcrumbs from my hands and step up to the counter.
"Can I help you?" I return her saccharine[9] stare with one of my own. She begins to speak so rapidly and without pause that I can't help wondering if she practices strategic breathing exercises.
"Hello dear how are you oh wonderful I will take three of your plain croissants and oh no dear not that one it looks overdone yes those ones to the left and also two of these delicious looking scones oh they are just to die for dear me you're so thin if I worked here well I would never be able to these wonderful treats would all be too hard to resist I need some bread what would you recommend never mind I will take a baguette – are the ones over here on this rack fresher than the ones you just gave me?"
It takes me a couple of seconds to realize she has stopped talking. I blink. "Actually, ma'am, they're all from the same batch[10], we just haven't had a chance to put those loaves on display."
"Oh well those look better than the ones you've got there so would you be a dear and put those back and give me the new ones oh thank you dear."
I do as she asks. I've worked at this bakery for four years, and in that time have learned that for our affluent[11] customers, the concepts of logic and sincerity are as foreign as the cleaning ladies they employ. It seems that reason and compassion[12] are qualities reserved for the working class.
I ring up her order at the register, and she walks out, high heels clicking. The stench[13] of her perfume lingers[14]. I turn to face Cassandra. We both smile.
"Can you believe some of the people who come in here?"
"I know, seriously." [...]

[8] loudly breathing out; [9] sweetener [10] made at the same time; [11] rich; [12] strong feeling of sympathy (Mitgefühl); [13] strong unpleasant smell; [14] here: stays after she has left the shop

Zusammenfassung *(summary)*

GOOD TO KNOW *How to write a summary*

Stelle die wichtigen **W-Fragen** an den Text:
- Wo spielt die Handlung?
- Wer sind die handelnden Personen?
- Was geschieht? Was tun die Personen? Warum? Wie? Mit welchen Folgen?

Schreibe einen **einleitenden Satz,** der aussagt, worum es im Text geht.
Gliedere den Text in kleine Häppchen:
- Unterteile den Text in Sinnabschnitte. Meist helfen dir dabei schon die Absätze des Textes.
- Fasse die einzelnen Sinnabschnitte mit wenigen eigenen Worten zusammen.

Reduziere deine Inhaltsangabe auf **das Wesentliche** (keine Ausschmückung, keine Details, keine wörtliche Rede).
Baue **keine Spannung** auf (kein verschachteltes Erzählen, kein *surprise ending,* keine Lücken, neutrale Wortwahl, d. h. Verzicht auf suddenly o. Ä., auf lautmalerische Wörter usw.).
In einer Inhaltsangabe erfolgt **keine Wertung.**
Schreibe im ***present tense***.

2 **Describe the encounter between the narrator and her customer.**
Diese Aufgabe entspricht der ersten Teilaufgabe der Textaufgabe (siehe Kasten S. 79).

Gehe in folgenden Schritten vor:
1. Schreibe deinen einleitenden Satz.
2. Schreibe einen Satz, der die Zeilen 1–7 zusammenfasst.
3. Schreibe einen Satz, der die Zeilen 8–15 zusammenfasst.
4. Schreibe einen Satz, der die Zeilen 16–26 zusammenfasst.
5. Fasse die Schlussfolgerung der Erzählerin zusammen.

Analyse *(analysis)*

GOOD TO KNOW *How to analyse a character*

Folgende Fragen helfen, eine Figur zu verstehen:
- Was sagt der Erzähler über die Figur?
- Wie (mit welchen Worten) sagt er das?
- Was sagen andere über die Figur?
- Was sagt sie über sich selbst?

- Wie objektiv ist das Gesagte? Beachte negativ und positiv belegte Wörter, d.h. Wörter mit schlechtem oder gutem Unterton.

Die Beantwortung dieser Fragen gibt uns Aufschluss über die **direkte** Charakterisierung einer Figur.

Genau so bedeutsam ist häufig die ***indirekte*** Charakterisierung:

- Wie handelt die Figur?
- Was sagt sie?
- Was für eine Sprache benutzt sie? Wie spricht sie?

3 Describe what the narrator so strongly dislikes about the lady.

Diese Aufgabe entspricht der zweiten Teilaufgabe (siehe Kasten S. 79).
Sammle die Textpassagen, die für die Bearbeitung der Aufgabe Aufschluss geben.
Ergänze die Tabelle in deinem Heft.

character's outward appearance	her way of speaking	her actions	what she says	what others say/do
thin lips, white teeth, too white; ...	speaks rapidly; words and phrases: dear ...	taps against the glass bakery counter; ...	compliments: ...	you saw her first, ...

GOOD TO KNOW *Analysis – vocabulary*

Folgende Formulierungen helfen dir, eine genaue Analyse zu schreiben:

to become clear	to show	outward appearance
to be obvious	to describe	choice of words
to be evident	to make use of	negative/positive connotation
to be a sign of	interjection	

thematic vocabulary

Die folgenden Wörter sind für die vorliegende Aufgabe nützlich:

dislike	annoying	compliment
overdone	impatient	false
impatience	never content	disgusting
command	never satisfied	

4 Now write an analysis.
Du kannst sie gemäß deiner bisherigen Antworten strukturieren. Die Anfänge der Abschnitte helfen dir dabei.

EXAMPLE

So könnten die Abschnitte deiner Analyse beginnen:
The assistants in the shop do not really want to serve the lady ("You saw her first, you deal with her") and the narrator turns to her with a sigh.
The narrator's dislike of the lady becomes apparent in her choice of words when she describes her.
Moreover, the narrator uses a large number of words with negative connotations. ...
The lady's behaviour reveals ...
The way she speaks is annoying ...
Even her compliments ...

Über den Text hinaus: Stellungnahme *(comment)*

GOOD TO KNOW *How to write a comment*

Sammle auf einem Konzeptpapier Argumente:
- pro und kontra oder
- für die eine oder andere Seite.

Finde Beispiele aus deiner eigenen Erfahrung,
- die deine persönliche Meinung unterstützen oder
- die entgegengesetzte Meinung widerlegen.

Beachte: Ein Argument besteht aus: **These – Begründung – Beispiel.**
Gelange dann zu einer Schlussfolgerung, zu einer fundierten eigenen Meinung.

5 "Reason and compassion are qualities reserved for the working class." (line 29–30) Do you agree?

Diese Aufgabe entspricht der Teilaufgabe 3 a) der Textaufgabe (siehe Kasten S. 79).
Trage Argumente für und gegen die Aussage zusammen und ziehe deine eigene Schlussfolgerung.
Beachte die Hinweise im Kasten „How to write a comment“ und bearbeite zunächst die folgende Aufgabe.

6 Find arguments that support or oppose the narrator's opinion.
Fill in the chart with arguments. Write in your exercise book.

no reason and compassion in higher classes		reason and compassion reserved to working class	
pros	**cons**	**pros**	**cons**
variety of choice fussy (pingelig) ... used to giving orders ... out of touch	education ...	...	...

7 Write your view of the statement in question 5.
In the box below you will find some useful expressions.

GOOD TO KNOW *Comment – useful vocabulary*

One could argue that ...
Thus, ...
This may lead to ...
They may be ...
However, ...
Education is to do with ...
Educated people should have learned ...
Furthermore, ...
You will find ...
Summing up, ...
I think / I am of the opinion / I hold the view / I definitely do not think ...

Kreative Schreibaufgabe *(creative task)*

GOOD TO KNOW *How to write a creative text*

Versetze dich in den fiktiven Schreiber des Textes.
- Wer ist er?
- Wie ist seine Sicht der Dinge?
- Was für eine Art Sprache benutzt er?

Knüpfe inhaltlich an die Erkenntnisse aus den Teilaufgaben 1 und 2 an.

8 **The assistant in the bookshop next door likes the lady and her behaviour. Write a short episode in which he/she describes the lady as she appears in the shop.**

Diese Aufgabe entspricht der Teilaufgabe 3 b) der Textaufgabe (siehe Kasten S. 79). Ersetze zunächst in deiner Liste der Aussagen über die Kundin aus Aufgabe 3 (S. 82) die negativ gefärbten Wörter durch positive, die denselben Sachverhalt beschreiben.

original choice of words (appearance)	contrasting positive words	original choice of words (way of speaking)	contrasting positive words
thin lips, white teeth, too white; pink, diseased, old-lady gums; unnatural smile; eyes too squinty and sparkling;	clean teeth friendly smile	speaks rapidly, repeats the same phrases: "Hello dear how are you oh wonderful ..." "... be a dear, oh thank you dear."	...
day-old mascara clings; expensive pantsuit; smells of perfume and old money; silk shirt; frail shoulders; baubles; spider-fingers; saccharine stare; high heels clicking; stench of her perfume.	...		

Nun schreibe die Erzählung des Buchhändlers.

EXAMPLE

So könntest du beginnen:

She is my favourite customer. ...

How to write about a text – tension

GOOD TO KNOW **Typische Aufgaben zu einem spannenden Text**

Der Schwerpunkt deiner Arbeit lag bei „Can I help you?“ auf der Charakterisierung. In der folgenden Textaufgabe geht es um Spannungserzeugung. Wie immer gilt: Die erste Teilaufgabe gibt den Inhalt wieder, die zweite Teilaufgabe beschreibt die Gestaltung des Textes, Teilaufgabe 3 wertet oder verlangt eine kreative Schreibaufgabe. (vgl. S. 78)
Hier siehst du die Aufgaben zu einem Auszug aus *The Wave* von Morton Rhue, die du nach dem Lesen bearbeiten sollst:

1. Sum up what happens to Laurie in Gordon High School one night.
2. Describe how the atmosphere in the school and certain key events add to Laurie's fear and thus create tension.
3. a) Comment on the problem of bullying in school life. Give examples from your everyday experience and state your personal view.
   b) Members of *The Wave* bully opponents of this movement. Write a letter to *The Grapevine* against such violence.

1 **Read the text carefully.**
You can also listen to the text on the CD.

The Wave

Track 9

Laurie is the editor-in-chief of the school magazine "The Grapevine". She has written a critical article against "The Wave", a new movement at her school which a large number of students are very enthusiastic about but which has turned out to be a danger to freedom of speech and thought.

As usual Laurie was the last one to leave the publications office. One thing about The Grapevine staff – they were great at parties, but when it became time to clean up, somehow they all disappeared. It had come as a shock to Laurie earlier that year when she realized what having the top position on the paper, editor-in-chief, really meant: having to do every little stupid job no one else wanted to do. And tonight that meant cleaning up

after the rest of the staff went home. By the time she finished, Laurie realized that it had already grown dark outside, and she was practically alone in the school building. As she closed the door of The Grapevine office and turned off the light, that nervousness she'd felt all week began to return again. The Wave was undoubtedly smarting[1] from the wounds The Grapevine had inflicted, but it was still strong in Gordon High, and Laurie was aware that as the head of the paper she ...
No, she told herself, you're just being silly and paranoid. The Wave was nothing serious, just a classroom experiment that had got slightly out of hand. There was nothing to be afraid of.
The corridors were darkened now, as Laurie headed to her locker to drop off a book she would not need that evening. The silence of the empty school was eerie[2]. For the first time she heard sounds she'd never heard before: the hums and buzzes of electrical current running to and from alarms and smoke detectors. A bubbling, splashing sound coming from the science room where some overnight experiment must have been left brewing. Even the unusually loud hollow echo of her own shoes as they rapped the hard corridor floors.
A few feet from her locker, Laurie froze. There on her locker door, the word 'enemy' was painted in red letters. Suddenly the loudest noise in the corridor was the quick, insistent beating of her own heart. Calm down, she told herself. Someone is just trying to scare you. She tried to get control of herself and started to do the combination of her lock. But she stopped in mid-turn. Had she heard something? Footsteps?
Laurie backed slowly away from her locker, gradually losing her battle to suppress her own growing fright. She turned and started walking down the hallway towards the exit. The sound of footsteps seemed to be growing louder, and Laurie quickened her pace. The footsteps grew even louder, and all at once the lights at the far end of the hall went out. Terrified, Laurie turned and peered back down into the dark hallway. Was that someone? Was there someone down there?
The next thing Laurie knew, she was running down the hallway towards the exit doors at the end. It seemed to take forever to get there, and when she finally reached the double metal doors and banged her hip against the opening bar, they were locked!
In a panic, Laurie threw herself against the next set of doors. Miraculously they opened, and she flew into the cool evening air, running and running.

[1] to feel pain; [2] unheimlich

Zusammenfassung *(summary)*

GOOD TO KNOW *How to write a summary*

Sieh dir den Kasten auf Seite 81 noch einmal an.
Denke daran: In einer Inhaltsangabe gibt es keine Spannung (kein verschachteltes Erzählen, kein *surprise ending*, keine Lücken, neutrale Wortwahl, d.h. Verzicht auf suddenly o.Ä., Verzicht auf lautmalerische Wörter, inneren Monolog, Fragen, usw.). Alles, was mit Spannung zu tun hat, gehört in Teilaufgabe 2 (in diesem Kapitel Aufgabe 3, S. 89).

2 Sum up what happens to Laurie in Gordon High School one night.
Diese Aufgabe entspricht der ersten Teilaufgabe der Textaufgabe (siehe Kasten S. 86). Write less than 100 words. To do this, complete the following sentences.

This excerpt from *The Wave* tells how Laurie ...
After her work ... Laurie ...
She wants to leave a book ...
When she gets to her ...
Then she thinks ...
Frightened, she runs ... and manages ...

Analyse *(analysis)*

GOOD TO KNOW *Atmosphere*

Atmosphere wird geschaffen durch die Beschreibung des *setting*, also des Schauplatzes der Geschichte.
Achte z. B. auf

- Aussehen
  - hell und dunkel
  - alt und neu
  - schmutzig und sauber
  - warm und kalt
  - schön und hässlich
- Farben
- Geräusche
- Stimmung *(mood)*

3 **Describe how the atmosphere in the school and certain key events add to Laurie's fear and thus create tension.**
Diese Aufgabe entspricht der zweiten Teilaufgabe der Textaufgabe (siehe Kasten S. 86). Bearbeite zur Erledigung dieser Teilaufgabe in kleinen Schritten die Aufgaben 4 bis 7.

4 **Find all the expressions in the text that describe the school building that evening.**
Ergänze die Tabelle in deinem Heft.

light	sounds	mood	other
dark	silence	alone	empty school
...		eerie	
		...	

5 **Write the part of your analysis concerned with atmosphere.**
Use the expressions from the table in 4 above.

EXAMPLE

You could start your analysis of the atmosphere like this:
The narrator creates an eerie atmosphere. Laurie is alone in the empty school. It is ...

GOOD TO KNOW *Plot*

Bestimmte ***key events*** in der Handlung steigern die Spannung immer weiter, bis sie einen Höhepunkt oder Wendepunkt erreicht und dann abfällt.

rising tension → climax or turning point → falling tension or relief

6 **Find the key events, climax and point of relief in the text.**

key events:

1. echoing footsteps
2. Laurie froze; the word "enemy" was painted ...
   ...

climax: ...
relief: ...

7 **Write the part of your analysis concerned with plot.**
Die folgenden Ausdrücke helfen dir.

The tension begins to grow when ...
It increases when ... and increases even more when ...
The next key event (line ...) is when ...
With ... the tension still rises.
The climax is reached in line ..., when ...
Finally the tension is relieved when ...

Über den Text hinaus: Stellungnahme *(comment)*

GOOD TO KNOW *How to write an expository comment*

Mach dir folgende Punkte klar:
- Was ist das Problem? Welche Fakten kannst du benennen?
- Welche Beispiele kannst du anführen?
- Welche Gründe für das Problem gibt es?
- Was sind mögliche Konsequenzen?

Gelange zu einer Schlussfolgerung, einer persönlichen Meinung.

Die folgenden Wörter und Ausdrücke helfen dir, einen Kommentar zu verfassen.

	is is regarded as is considered	a serious problem
I know In my school there are In my town In my family	a lot of cases of a lot of examples of many people many students	...
For example Another example A further example	...	
In the case of What happened is that	...	
Possible reasons A possible reason The obvious reason	are/is may be could be	the ... the fact that there are ... the fact that more and more ...

The consequences are obvious: If this situation does not change	society will ... our schools may... we will ... students may	
To my mind In my opinion In my view	we should ... politicians should ... parents should ... schools should ...	
To sum up To conclude	...	

8 **Comment on the problem of bullying in school life. Give examples from your everyday experience and state your personal view.**

Diese Aufgabe entspricht der Teilaufgabe 3 a) der Textaufgabe (siehe Kasten S. 86). Anders als bei „Can I help you?“ geht es hier nicht um gegensätzliche Meinungen, sondern um eine wertende Darstellung.

EXAMPLE

You could start your comment like this:

Laurie is bullied for her different opinion, which she has stated in the school magazine. But every day students are bullied for a number of other reasons, too. ...

Kreative Schreibaufgabe *(creative task)*

GOOD TO KNOW *How to write a letter to a newspaper*

Gliedere deinen Brief wie folgt:
Anrede: Sir oder Madam, kein Dear (gilt nicht bei einer Schülerzeitung)
Was ist der Grund deines Briefes?
Welche Situation/Ereignisse haben dich zum Schreiben veranlasst?
Gründe für diese Ereignisse? Konsequenzen?
Wie ist deine Meinung dazu?
Appelliere an die Leser!
Unterschrift: nur dein Name

GOOD TO KNOW *Writing a letter to a newspaper – useful vocabulary*

I'm writing to you because ...
incidents we can't accept
new movement
to be fascinated with
Basically it is a good thing ...
to get organized, to follow a common goal
In this case, however, ...
attack
to intimidate
we can't accept
basic ideals of our country
freedom of speech
free press
think twice about
support

9 Members of *The Wave* bully opponents of this movement. Write a letter to *The Grapevine* against such violence.
Diese Aufgabe entspricht der Teilaufgabe 3 b) der Textaufgabe (siehe Kasten S. 86). Die Wörter und Ausdrücke in dem Kasten helfen dir bei der Lösung der Aufgabe.

EXAMPLE

You could write your letter, for example, starting like this:
Dear Editors, dear Gordon High Students,
I'm writing to you because there have been incidents in our school ...

Test

Du solltest nun in der Lage sein, die folgende Schreibaufgabe selbstständig zu bearbeiten.
Die Bewertung bezieht sich auf die inhaltlichen Aspekte der Antworten.
Die Textaufgabe ist in die folgenden Teilaufgaben gegliedert:

1. Briefly outline how the relationship between the boy and the girl develops.
2. Describe the behaviour of the boy, the girl, and their classmates. How does it show that the boy and girl are outsiders in their class? How does the boy's behaviour change?
3. a) Outsiders may have serious problems with their classmates. Can you find ways of helping them?
   b) Tell the story from the boy's point of view.

1 Read the text.
You can also listen to the text on the CD.

Hidden Blue — Track 10

By Misha H.

He steps into the classroom with his head down, almost ashamed to be here. He walks quickly to the back to an old chemical-stained desk, but his effort doesn't work. The jocks[1] notice him and begin to pull puns[2]. His head lowers with each throbbing[3] word.
He is the smartest guy in the school and is often used as a model student in class. Each time he is mentioned, classmates turn and stare while his head lowers to its limit. He barely looks up, only to take notes from the chalk-caked board.
He looks at me and I smile. He turns his head, lowering it again, and begins to write. I wonder if it hurts him more than it hurts me. People smile and act kind, but they make fun of him. People smile at me, but I shrug it off.
I'm an outcast among the girls. I'm not a shopper or a rich girl who flaunts[4] dim-witted[5] talent. I sit by myself, and I'm the subject of gossip[6] and cruelty, but I'm not as smart as him. I can't say that I feel sorry for him for being mocked because he's the smartest guy around. I feel sorry for the others who don't notice his traits. He is smarter than everyone here, and he is kinder. I think his best trait is his hidden blue eyes.
His deep blue eyes are darker than the sea, and Poseidon[7] could never possess them. No other person in the school has eyes like his. They're always covered by his thick black hair which drifts down to his neck. I notice them every day and they haven't ceased to enthrall[8] me.

[1] athlete; [2] to make jokes; [3] to beat, to hit; [4] to show off with; [5] stupid; [6] talk;
[7] Greek god of the sea; [8] to fascinate

Class ends and he quickly leaves, his normal routine to avoid confrontation. I smile at him every day; I wonder if he notices.
Another day, another class, and with it come more words. He steps into the room with his head high. He walks slowly to the back and sits next to me. Everyone glares at his unusual behavior and takes off in conversation and gossip. I can't help but smile as he stares at me during class.
Class ends, and gossip stirs. He stands as I stand, and I look at him with a smile. He smiles in return, which makes his eyes gleam. He leans over and whispers, "You have gorgeous green eyes."

2 Briefly outline how the relationship between the boy and the girl develops. (Teilaufgabe 1)

Your points: ____ /5

3 Describe the behaviour of the boy, the girl, and their classmates. How does it show that the boy and girl are outsiders in their class? How does the boy's behaviour change? (Teilaufgabe 2)

Your points: ____ /5

4 Outsiders may have serious problems with their classmates. Can you find ways of helping them? (Teilaufgabe3 a)

Your points: ____ /4

5 Tell the story from the boy's point of view. (Teilaufgabe 3 b)

Your points: ____ /6

Your total points out of 20 points: ____

- More than 17? Very good.
- More than 15? Good.
- Less than 10? Have a look at this chapter again.
  You CAN do better.

3.2 Über Sachtexte *(non-fiction)* schreiben

REMEMBER Aufbau von Textaufgaben – Sachtexte

Wenn du in einer Klassenarbeit oder Prüfung über einen Sachtext schreiben musst, wird dir fast immer ein fertiger Text (Ausgangstext) vorgegeben.
In der Regel wird die erste Teilaufgabe zu einer Schreibaufgabe überprüfen, ob du den Inhalt des Ausgangstextes verstanden hast. Meist wirst du aufgefordert, eine ***summary*** des Textes zu schreiben.
Im Anschluss daran folgt eine **Analyse-Aufgabe**, bei der z. B. ein im Text beschriebenes Problem oder der Aufbau des Textes analysiert werden soll.
Die dritte Teilaufgabe geht auch hier über den Text hinaus: Entweder wird eine **Stellungnahme** gefordert oder eine **kreative Schreibaufgabe.**

Beispiel:
Hier siehst du eine Aufgabenstellung für den folgenden Text „Schools warned of pupils hooked on energy drinks", die in diesem Kapitel Schritt für Schritt gelöst wird:

1. Summarize the information which the text "Schools warned of pupils hooked on energy drinks" gives on the problem of schoolchildren's use of energy drinks.
2. Analyse how the author uses experts' opinions in her article.
3. a) Should children try to improve their school performance through the use of energy drinks or caffeine tablets? Give arguments for both sides and state your own position.
   b) Write a letter to an "Agony Aunt".

How to write about a text – non-fictional texts

1 **Read the text carefully.**
You can also listen to the text on the CD.

Schools warned of pupils hooked on[1] energy drinks — Track 11

By Polly Curtis, The Guardian, September 3, 2008

Children are becoming dependent on energy drinks that have dramatic effects on their concentration and behaviour in school, drug experts have warned. Schools are being advised to observe children for signs of agitation[2] which could be a result of excessive[3] caffeine consumption. It follows reports of pupils drinking large quantities of energy drinks or taking caffeine-based[4] pills.

[1] abhängig sein von; [2] Aufregung, Erregung; [3] übermäßig; [4] mit Koffein;

The warning, from the anti-drugs advisory group[5] Drug Education UK, comes as ministers prepare to unveil[6] new measures[7] tomorrow to improve school dinners and advise parents on children's packed lunches.

Bob Tait, from Drug Education UK, said: "There is a growing problem of caffeine abuse in schools. Most schools have a drug education programme to advise kids against illegal drugs, but there is less known about legal highs[8]." He gave his warning at a conference of school nurses this week, the *Nursing Times* reported.

Tait said: "Children will drink them on the walk to school, at break and lunch time. If you have got a child who is worked up on[9] an energy drink, they are going to be agitated during lesson time." Energy drinks contain up to 160 mg of caffeine per can, while tablets can contain 50 mg of caffeine per tablet. They are said to combat[10] tiredness, improve performance and boost[11] concentration. Tait singled out[12] Bruzz as a particular problem.

Malcolm Trobe, head of Malmesbury School in Wiltshire until last term and now policy director[13] of the Association of School and College Leaders[14], said: "Schools are concerned about the abuse of energy drinks. What is clear is students use them at exam time, if they are staying up late and revising or if they've got a lot of exams on one day."

Margaret Morrissey, of the National Confederation of Parent Teacher Associations[15], said: "These drinks are often marketed to help pupils through exams. It means we are teaching children early to have addictions, when any average young person with an average lifestyle does not need an energy drink to make it through the day."

A Bruzz spokesman said: "In general, children are more sensitive[16] to caffeine than adults. This is why we do not recommend[17] Bruzz to caffeine-sensitive individuals, including children."

[5] Anti-Drogen Beratungsgruppe [6] enthüllen; [7] Maßnahmen; [8] hier: (legaler) Drogentrip; [9] aufgeregt sein von/wegen; [10] bekämpfen; [11] etwas ansteigen lassen; [12] jemanden/etwas herausgreifen; [13] Leiter der Strategieabteilung; [14] Leaders = headmasters and headmistresses (Schulleiter und Schulleiterinnen); [15] National Confederation of Parent Teacher Associations: Nationale Vereinigung von Eltern-Lehrer Verbänden: [16] empfindlich; [17] empfehlen

GOOD TO KNOW *Understanding non-fictional texts*

A first idea
Um eine erste Vorstellung davon zu bekommen, worum es in dem Ausgangstext geht, sieh dir zunächst nur die Überschrift, das Bild und (falls vorhanden) die Bildunterschrift an. Sie geben Hinweise auf den Inhalt des Textes.

Schlüsselbegriffe finden
Nachdem du eine erste Vorstellung vom Inhalt des Texts bekommen hast, lies den ganzen Text und markiere die Schlüsselbegriffe.

Die Struktur des Arguments erkennen
Um zu erkennen, wie der Konsum von „energy drinks“ in der Schule hier dargestellt wird, musst du versuchen, die Informationen, Meinungen und Argumente des Zeitungsartikels zu ordnen. Benutze die vorgegebene Textstruktur (Abschnitte), um die Informationen des Textes zu ordnen. Versuche zunächst, für jeden Abschnitt eine Überschrift zu finden. Mache dann eine Tabelle der Argumente für und gegen „energy drinks“ in der Schule. So wirst du leicht erkennen, ob die Autorin einseitig oder eher unparteiisch an die Sache herangeht. Daraus kannst du erschließen, ob sie schon erwartet, dass die Leser und Leserinnen mit ihr übereinstimmen oder ob sie davon ausgeht, dass diese mit (komplexerer) Argumentation überzeugt werden müssen. In diesem Schritt gehen Analyse und Bewertung Hand in Hand.

Personen und Aussagen einander zuordnen
Wenn in einem Text (oft werden es Sachtexte sein) verschiedene Sichtweisen auf ein Problem dargestellt werden, kann es hilfreich sein, diese Sichtweisen den Personen zuzuordnen, die sie vertreten. Manchmal bezieht sich eine Aufgabenstellung auch genau darauf, die Sichtweise einer Person oder mehrerer Personen zu bearbeiten.

Informationen aus dem Text sammeln und sortieren
Schreibe alle Informationen und Argumente zu dem im Text behandelten Problem heraus und sortiere sie in die entsprechenden Spalten der Tabelle ein.

2 Complete the following sentence.
Just from looking at the headline, the photograph and the caption I think the article deals with ...

3 Complete the table with key words from the text.

Headline	schools warned	___ ___	energy drinks			
Paragraph 1	children becoming ___	concentration	behaviour	signs of ___	excessive ___ ___	
Paragraph 2	new government ___					
Paragraph 3	growing problem	drug education ___	illegal drugs	___		
Paragraph 4	way to school ___ ___	drinks: ___ mg caffeine	tablets: ___ mg caffeine	combat tiredness	improve ___ ___	Bruzz particular problem
Paragraph 5	schools concerned	___ of energy drinks	___ ___			
Paragraph 6	___ to help through exams	schools teaching ___	average person	average ___	no need for energy drinks	
Paragraph 7	Bruzz spokesman	children more ___ to caffeine	don't ___ ___ to children			

4 Match each of the following headings to a paragraph of the text.

	Heading	lines
1	Caffeine-sensitive people should avoid caffeine	___ – ___
2	Pupils become dependent on energy drinks	___ – ___
3	Schools only know how to deal with illegal drugs	___ – ___
4	Energy drinks as helpers in times of exam pressure	___ – ___
5	Schools teach children to develop addiction	___ – ___
6	Government advising on school food	___ – ___
7	Tait warns on the when, where and what of energy drinks and caffeine tablets	___ – ___

5 Match the following statements to the person who makes them.

A – Bob Tait
B – Malcolm Trobe
C – Margaret Morissey
D – Bruzz spokesman

Person	Statement
	... children are more sensitive to caffeine than adults.
	... we are teaching children early to have addictions.
	... we do not recommend Bruzz to ... children.
	... students use them at exam time, if they are staying up late revising ...
	Children will drink them ... at break or lunch time.
	Schools are concerned about the abuse of energy drinks.
	There is a growing problem of caffeine abuse in schools.
	These drinks are often marketed to help pupils through exams.

6 Make a table of positive and negative aspects of energy drinks as seen in this text.
Lege in deinem Heft eine Tabelle an. Die Tabelle sollte die beiden Spalten „positive aspects“ und „negative/critical aspects“ haben.

Zusammenfassung *(summary)*

GOOD TO KNOW *How to write a summary*

Jetzt hast du einen geordneten Überblick über die wichtigsten inhaltlichen Aspekte des Texts und kannst mit dem Schreiben der *summary* beginnen.
Beim Schreiben einer *summary* solltest du genau auf die Formulierung der Aufgabenstellung achten.

REMEMBER *Writing a summary – getting started*

Für die Bearbeitung einer zusammenfassenden Inhaltsaufgabe wird oft ein einleitender Satz erwartet. Dieser sollte folgende Angaben enthalten:

- Titel
- Verfasser
- Erscheinungszeit, -ort und -medium (z. B. Name einer Tageszeitung)
- Textformat (z. B. Zeitungsartikel)
- allgemeine Formulierung des Kernthemas

1 Which introductory sentence is most suitable for a summary of the "energy drinks" article?

1. "Schools warned of pupils hooked on energy drinks" is about Bruzz in schools.
2. The newspaper article "Schools warned of pupils hooked on energy drinks", written by Polly Curtis, is about energy drinks.
3. The text "Schools warned of pupils hooked on energy drinks", written by Polly Curtis and published in *The Guardian*, September 3, 2008 deals with energy drinks.
4. "Schools warned of pupils hooked on energy drinks", written by Polly Curtis, published in The Guardian, September 3, 2008, is about energy drinks.
5. The article "Schools warned of pupils hooked on energy drinks", by Polly Curtis, published in *The Guardian*, September 3, 2008, is about the dangers of energy drinks for schoolchildren.

GOOD TO KNOW *Writing a summary – full text version*

Jetzt solltest du soweit vorbereitet sein, dass du die *summary* (Teilaufgabe 1) schreiben kannst. Wende dabei die Dinge an, die du in den vorherigen Arbeitschritten gelernt hast.
Ein zusammenfassender Text darf im Vergleich zum Ausgangstext nicht zu lang sein. Grundsätzlich werden die *summary*-Aufgaben in den Zeitformen der Gegenwart geschrieben.

Hier folgt eine Übersicht mit nützlichen Ausdrücken für eine Zusammenfassung:

The newspaper article ...	is about ... deals with ...
The author draws attention to the fact that ... The author points out ... The author goes on to show how ...	

The text The author	also mentions ...
Finally, the author refers to ...	

2 **Summarize the information on the problem of schoolchildren's use of energy drinks given in the text "Schools warned of pupils hooked on energy drinks".**
Do not write more than 150 words.
Diese Aufgabe entspricht der ersten Teilaufgabe der Textaufgabe (s. Kasten S. 95).

Analyse *(analysis)*

GOOD TO KNOW — *How to understand the text structure*

Nun folgt die Teilaufgabe 2 der Textaufgabe.
Beispiel für eine typische Aufgabenstellung für Teilaufgabe 2:
Analyse how the author of this article presents the problem of energy drinks and schoolchildren.

In dieser Art von Aufgabe geht es darum, einzelne Aspekte eines Textes zu analysieren. Dazu gehört z. B., dass du die Aussageabsicht und den Aufbau des Textes erkennen und darüber schreiben kannst.

Sprache beschreiben – Wirkabsichten erkennen
Für die genannte Aufgabenstellung bedeutet dies, dass du ein Gestaltungsmerkmal des Ausgangstextes darstellen sollst. Das soll allerdings nicht in Form einer Beschreibung geschehen. Der Auftrag besteht darin, die Absicht der Autorin, die sich hinter dieser konkreten Gestaltung verbirgt, zu erkennen und zu benennen.
In Prüfungsaufgaben sollst du oft nur **ein** Gestaltungsmittel behandeln, das der Autor verwendet. Für die Textform „Zeitungsartikel" findest du auf S. 102 eine Übersicht der wichtigsten Elemente. Jedes dieser Elemente könnte Gegenstand einer Prüfungsaufgabe sein.

Zeitungsartikel – *Newspaper Articles*
Mit ihren Zeitungsartikeln wollen die Autoren die Leser informieren bzw. zu deren Meinungsbildung beitragen. Deshalb muss beim Leser ein Leseinteresse geweckt und aufrecht erhalten werden *(catching and keeping the reader's attention)*.

Um ihre Ziele zu erreichen, benutzen die Autoren verschiedene Verfahren. Die Aufgabenstellung verlangt von dir, diese Verfahren und ihre beabsichtigten Wirkungen darzustellen.

Wichtige Verfahren bzw. Elemente beim Verfassen von Zeitungsartikeln sind z. B.:
- die Überschrift – *headline (eye-catcher)*
- Bilder und Bildunterschriften – *captions*
- die sprachliche Gestaltung des Artikels (Wortschatz, Grammatik, besondere Sprachformen)
- Aufbau/Struktur des Artikels
- Zitate von Experten oder Betroffenen

1 Which words in the headline have most impact?
Sieh dir die Überschrift des Artikels an und überlege, welches der dort verwendeten Wörter welchen Aufmerksamkeitsgrad beim Leser auslöst. Trage die Werte in die Tabelle ein.

word	level of interest				
	1	2	3	4	5
Schools					
warned of					
pupils					
hooked on					
energy drinks					

2 What sort of words and expressions occur most frequently in the text?
Zähle, wie oft im Text Wörter aus den folgenden Bereichen im Text vorkommen:

category	number of occurrences
“dealing with a threat” or “giving a warning”	
“increase” or “become more important/serious”	
“drug abuse and addiction”	

3 Check alternative verb forms in the first paragraph for impact.
Vergleiche die drei Versionen des ersten Abschnitts des Artikels.
Kreuze die Version an, in der die verwendeten Verbformen am deutlichsten auf die Aktualität und Brisanz des Problems hinweisen.

1. Children often become dependent on energy drinks that can have dramatic effects on their concentration and behaviour in school, drug experts warned.
2. Children often become dependent on energy drinks that have dramatic effects on their concentration and behaviour in school, drug experts warn.
3. Children are becoming dependent on energy drinks that have dramatic effects on their concentration and behaviour in school, drug experts have warned.

4 What use does the text make of expert opinion?

Aus den vorangegangenen Aufgaben weißt du, dass die Autorin in ihrem Text Expertenmeinungen zitiert.
Stelle fest

▷ wie Bob Tait, Malcolm Trobe, Margaret Morissey und der Vertreter von Bruzz als Experten ausgewiesen werden,

▷ wie hoch der Anteil der Expertenzitate am Gesamttext ist.

Welchen Effekt erzielt die Autorin durch ihre Art, mit den Expertenmeinungen umzugehen?

5 Find key points to show how the author presents the question of energy drinks in schools.

▷ In den Aufgaben 1 und 2 hast du herausgefunden, dass Wörter aus dem Wortfeld „Warnung" im Text häufig vorkommen. Überlege, was es für den Leser z. B. bedeutet, ganz am Anfang des Textes zu lesen: „drug experts have warned".

▷ Sieh dir noch mal die Ergebnisse der Aufgabe 6 des vorigen Abschnitts (S. 99) und Aufgabe 4 oben an. Zähle die positiven und negativen Argumente nochmals auf, und untersuche, ob positive Ausdrücke ohne kritischen Kommentar bleiben. Untersuche, ob Expertenmeinungen ein eher einseitiges oder ausgeglichenes Bild abgeben.

▷ Anzahl der positiven Aspekte ohne kritische Ergänzung:

▷ Anzahl der positiven Expertenmeinungen:
Frage auch, ob die Autorin eine nüchterne oder eher emotionale Sprache benutzt. Warum – wie wirkt ihr Sprachstil?

▷ Überlege, ob die Autorin erwartet, dass ihre Leserinnen und Leser ihre Meinung teilen. Meint sie, gegen starke Gegenmeinungen kämpfen zu müssen, wo sie komplexere Argumente geben und ihre eigene Meinung kräftiger darstellen müsste, oder stellt sie die Sache als ohnehin schon entschieden dar?

▷ Notiere dir, was die vermutlichen Gegner sagen – die, die ein eindeutiges Interesse an den Verkauf von „energy drinks" an Schulkinder haben.

Wenn du das alles gemacht hast, schreibe einen kurzen Absatz, der deine Ergebnisse präsentiert.

6 Analyse how the author uses experts' opinions in her article.
Diese Aufgabe entspricht der zweiten Teilaufgabe der Textaufgabe (s. Kasten S. 95). Präsentiere nun die Ergebnisse der vorangegangen Aufgaben 1 bis 5 in einem zusammenhängenden Text.

Über den Text hinaus: **Stellungnahme (*comment*)**

GOOD TO KNOW — **Stellungnahme und kreative Schreibaufgabe**

Die dritte Teilaufgabe geht meist deutlich über die Grenzen eines Ausgangstextes hinaus. Hier musst du selbstständig einen Text zur Thematik schreiben. Oft hast du hier die Wahl zwischen einer kommentierenden Stellungnahme oder auch Diskussion und einer kreativen Schreibaufgabe - z. B. einem privaten (Leser-) Brief, einem Tagebucheintrag, einer E-Mail, einem offiziellen, förmlichen Brief, einem Lebenslauf, einer Bewerbung o. Ä.
Bei den kreativen Schreibaufgaben ist es besonders wichtig, die formalen Vorgaben für diese Texte zu beachten, z. B. Anrede- und Schlussformeln (Briefe), Layout-Vorgaben (z. B. Zeitungs- oder Magazinartikel), Autorenperspektive usw.

Die Teilaufgabe 3 für den Text über „energy drinks“ lautet folgendermaßen:

3 a) Should children try to improve their school performance through the use of energy drinks or caffeine tablets? Give arguments for both sides and state your own position.
b) Write a letter to an “Agony Aunt”.

Schau dir noch einmal den Kasten „How to write a comment“ auf S. 83 an. Dort findest du Hinweise, wie du Argumente sammelst und anordnest.

1 Should children try to improve their school performance through the use of energy drinks or caffeine tablets? Give arguments for both sides and state your own position.

Die Aufgabe entspricht der Teilaufgabe 3 a) der Textaufgabe.
Um diese Aufgabe zu lösen, bearbeite sie Schritt für Schritt.

GOOD TO KNOW *Writing your comment step by step*

Step 1: Collect ideas and arguments – make a list or mindmap.

Hier findest du eine Ideen- und Argumentensammlung mit Stichpunkten für die oben genannte Teilaufgabe 3 a):

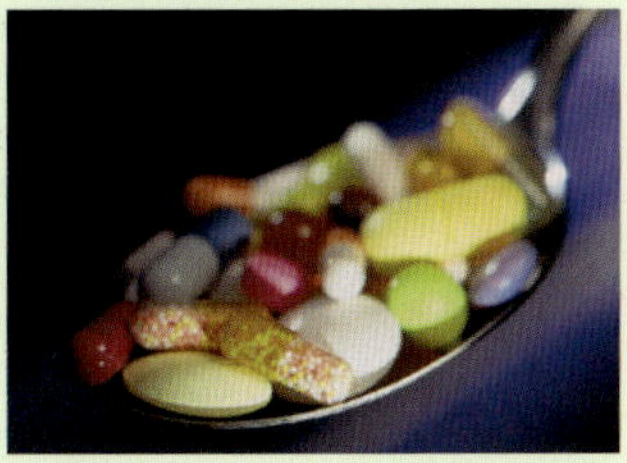

- the better the exam results, the more chances in life
- caffeine can help and it is legal
- boosting your school performance isn't doping or cheating – there is no principle of fair play involved, nor are there any spectators
- caffeine is part of our daily life anyway
- the stimulants' positive effects are only short-term
- there are long-term dangers: addiction and physical damage/bodily harm
- there are negative side-effects which are counterproductive: lack of concentration in class – more difficulty revising – need for more stimulants
- exams are set for the average pupil to pass – no huge effort/stimulants needed
- continuous work helps/reduces last-minute pressure
- personal success without stimulants boosts self-confidence
- I wouldn't take the risk

Step 2: Arrange and link the arguments.

Im nächsten Arbeitsschritt sollst du deine Argumente verbinden und so zu einem vollständig formulierten Text kommen. Verwende die Argumente, die du für Aufgabe 1 notiert hast, und benutze die folgenden Formulierungen:

Expressions for linking arguments:

First, you have to think of ...
To begin with I would like to state ...
In the first place we must consider ...
Then we can turn our attention to ...
Secondly, there are those who ...
Thirdly, we have to take into consideration ...
Similarly, you could argue that ...
Perhaps the most important point is ...
Furthermore, one could suggest ...
Moreover, if this isn't stopped, ...

Besides, there are the long-term effects ...
In addition to that, we have to see ...
Finally, I would like to stress ...

Expressions for opposing arguments:
However, looking at the disadvantages ...
Although this seems to be a good point, ...
In contrast to this there are the immense costs to consider ...
Alternatively, you could say ...
On the other hand you might want to point to the fact that ...
Nevertheless, we should not forget ...
Whereas from the consumer's point of view ...

Step 3: Write a concluding paragraph.
Am Ende der Argumentation sollte die klar erkennbare, persönliche Stellungnahme stehen. Du kannst die folgenden Ausdrücke als Satzanfänge verwenden:

Expressions for reaching a conclusion:
So we can quite rightly assume ...
Consequently, there is little point in ...
Thus, we need not rely on stimulants in order to ...
Therefore, I do not think it is a good idea to ...
As a result we may find ourselves in much more trouble ...
In conclusion, there seems to be little good to come from ...
All things considered, I think it is obvious that the only solution can be ...
Taking all these points into consideration, there is little choice other than to ...
All in all, we are faced with a situation in which ...
To sum up, we can put it like this: ...
As I see it, this is the real problem: ...
In my view/opinion, the answer must be ...
To cut a long story short, drugs are not the answer.

Schreibe nun deine Stellungnahme.

Kreative Schreibaufgabe (*creative task*)

GOOD TO KNOW *How to write a letter (to an Agony Aunt)*

In englischsprachigen Zeitschriften gibt es häufig eine Rubrik, in der Leserbriefe abgedruckt sind, in denen jemand um Hilfe bei einem persönlichen Problem bittet. Die Briefe werden von einer so genannten „Agony Aunt“ beantwortet: jemand, der die Rolle einer älteren Dame oder ‚Tante‘ einnimmt, die freundliche Ratschläge gibt. Wenn du einen solchen Brief schreiben möchtest, schreibst du ihn wie einen persönlichen Brief an Bekannte oder Freunde.

Die wichtigsten formalen Elemente des persönlichen Briefes sind:

- eigener Name
- Datum
- Ort
- angemessene Anrede (bei Agony Aunt meist Dear + Name, da aunt eine gewisse Vertrautheit ausdrückt)
- angemessene Grußformel am Ende

Du solltest dein Anliegen oder die Problemlage und deine Bedürfnisse oder Wünsche klar formulieren. Achte darauf, dein Anliegen überzeugend, aber nicht übertrieben darzustellen.

1 Write a letter to an Agony Aunt.

One of your friends seems to be nervous and stressed out. She or he has told you they don't sleep much because there's so much work for the exams, but they refuse to discuss the matter further with you. You suspect that they have a problem with caffeine, because you have seen them drinking a lot of energy drinks lately. You decide to write a letter to your youth magazine's Agony Aunt and ask for advice.

- Schreibe jetzt deinen Brief.
- Versuche danach, deinen Text mithilfe des Selbsteinschätzungsbogens (S. 108) zu beurteilen und zu überarbeiten. Überlege, ob du alle genannten Punkte bearbeitet hast. Wenn du unsicher bist, lass deinen Artikel von einer anderen Person bewerten.
- Suche dir einen kompetenten Sprecher, dem du deinen ausformulierten Text und den ausgefüllten Bogen geben kannst. Das können deine Eltern sein, ein älterer Schüler oder dein Lehrer.

A letter to an "Agony Aunt" – self-assessment and teacher/peer-assessment

formal aspects/style	**yes**	**no**
your own address	☐	☐
date	☐	☐
addressee's name and address	☐	☐
appropriate salutation	☐	☐
text written in clear, simple language	☐	☐
suitable closing formula	☐	☐
content		
problem clearly described	☐	☐
convincing presentation	☐	☐
request clearly stated	☐	☐

language features used	**always**	**sometimes**	**never**
correct use of irregular verb forms			
correct formation of questions			
correct formation of negations			
correct formation of complex sentences, if-clauses, relative clauses			
active/passive verb forms			
simple verb forms and -ing-forms			

language	**number of mistakes**
grammar	☐
SVO (Satzbau)	☐
verbs (including irregular verbs)	☐
questions	☐
negations	☐
other	☐

words used	**always**	**sometimes**	**never**
correct word			
variety of expression			
range of words			

Test

Du solltest nun in der Lage sein, die folgende Schreibaufgabe selbstständig zu bearbeiten. Die Bewertung bezieht sich auf die inhaltlichen Aspekte der Antworten. Du kannst den Text auch auf der CD hören.

Why we should step in to halt bad behaviour

Track 12

By Michael Hann, The Guardian, September 3, 2008

My wife thinks I'll get stabbed[1] one day. She thinks I get too angry about things I should let pass; she suspects that offering advice to those failing to observe basic social niceties is more provocative than helpful. She's not sure what I achieve by asking people to pick up their litter, or grabbing shoplifters, or asking a man in the doorway of McDonald's to stop hitting his girlfriend.

Part of me thinks she's right, and that my blood pressure would fall if I turned away. But then another side – for the sake of argument, let's call it a conscience – kicks in. The things I get mad about diminish[2] our society and lower the quality of life. Isn't it my duty to pipe up[3]?

In fact, shouldn't more people intervene? After all, isn't the well-being of society the responsibility of the whole of society?

It turns out I'm not alone. The think tank *Reform* says Britons are too ready to abdicate[4] responsibility for dealing with wrongdoing – that we have "nationalised and politicised" antisocial behaviour to such an extent that we have become a "nation of bystanders", six out of 10 of us would not step in to stop a group of teenage vandals. We think our duties end with calling the police; in other European countries tackling antisocial behaviour is seen as everyone's responsibility.

We do turn our backs because – like my wife – we believe the likely consequence of any intervention will be a stabbing. This despite the British Crime Survey showing that knife crime has remained stable over the past decade, and a Metropolitan Police survey showing that knife crime in London has actually dropped over the past two years, by a startling[5] 15.7%.

The saddest thing for those of us who believe it is right to intervene is that we get branded[6] as rightwing, law-and-order-obsessed vigilantes[7]. In fact, we're trying to uphold the classic leftwing value: that we are all responsible for the society we live in. It's not,

[1] (to) stab: stechen, erstechen; [2] diminish: verkleinern, wertloser machen; [3] (to) pipe up: sich zu Wort melden; [4] (to) abdicate: hier: sich verabschieden von, verzichten auf; [5] startling: überraschend [6] branded: wörtlich: mit dem Brandzeichen versehen, hier: bezeichnet als; [7] vigilante: Bürgerwehr

whatever David Cameron[8] might say, the Labour[9] government that's to blame for the I'll-do-what-I-want culture that most of us blame for antisocial behaviour. After all, it wasn't a Labour prime minister who said, "There's no such thing as society[10]," was it?

[8] David Cameron: 2008 führender britischer Politiker der Konservativen Partei, später britischer Premierminister; [9] Labour (party): (britische) Arbeiterpartei; [10] Das Zitat stammt von der ehemaligen britischen Premierministerin Margaret Thatcher von der Konservativen Partei (*Woman's Own*, Oktober 1987).

1 Sum up the main arguments for and against personal intervention in cases of anti-social behaviour.

Your points: ____ /8

2 What typical elements of a newspaper article does the author use to bring his view of the problem home to the reader?

Your points: ____ /9

3 a) You are travelling on a bus, local train or other means of local transport and you witness a violent attack on another passenger. Would you intervene in some way or try not to notice? Discuss.

Your points: ____ /7

b) Your school wants to hold a "Get-Involved Week". Write a text for a flyer in which you point out how important it is to fight anti-social behaviour.

Your points: ____ /5

Auf S. 111 folgt ein Selbsteinschätzungsbogen, der dir zeigt, welche Punkte bei einer Bewertung wichtig sind. Du kannst deine Lösungen wieder einer anderen Person, z. B. deiner Lehrerin oder deinem Lehrer, zur Beurteilung geben.

Your total points out of 29 points: ____

- More than 24? Very good.
- More than 21? Good.
- Less than 14? Have a look at this chapter again. You CAN do better.

A flyer – self-assessment and teacher/peer-assessment

formal aspects/style	**yes**	**no**
headings		
text divided into sections		
each section subdivided into appropriate items		
text written in clear, simple language		
flyer has impact on reader		
content		
five W-questions: Who is the flyer addressed to? What is it about? Why? When is the event? Where is the event?		
problem/facts/situation described clearly		

language features used	**always**	**sometimes**	**never**
correct use of irregular verb forms			
correct formation of questions			
correct formation of negations			
correct use of infinitives, gerunds and participles			
correct use of if-clauses			
active/passive verb forms			
simple forms and -ing-forms			

language	**number of mistakes**
grammar	
SVO (Satzbau)	
verbs (including irregular verbs)	
questions	
negations	
other	

words used	**always**	**sometimes**	**never**
correct word			
variety of words			
variety of expression			

Stichwortverzeichnis

Besser in

Englisch Lösungsheft

10. Klasse

Realschule

Cornelsen SCRIPTOR

1 Revision: Sprache verstehen

1.1 *The passive*

Exercise 1 Seite 6

1. is ... called
2. is broken into – is attacked – is not helped
3. Is ... justified?
4. are not trained
5. is reported
6. is examined – is collected
7. are ... treated
8. is made – are asked

Exercise 2 Seite 7

1. My parrot is being frightened by your cat. 2. He is being treated with contempt. 3. The (computer) software is now being updated. 4. Two men are being questioned by the police about the incident. 5. Money is being stolen from the lockers in the changing room. 6. I am being made fun of by those two girls over there. 7. A stage for the open-air concert is being erected.

Exercise 3 Seite 8

1. Boarding cards must be shown at the gate.
   Boarding cards are to be shown at the gate.
2. The emergency landing drill will be explained by a flight attendant.
   The emergency landing drill is to be explained by a flight attendant.
3. Valuables should be placed in the hotel safe.
   Valuables are to be placed in the hotel safe.
4. A visitor's pass must be displayed by all visitors.
   A visitor's pass is to be displayed by all visitors.
5. Annual fees must be paid by December 31.
   Annual fees are to be paid by December 31.
6. A model answer can be found at the end of the unit.
   A model answer is to be found at the end of the unit.
7. Her stories shouldn't be taken too seriously.
   Her stories aren't to be taken too seriously.
8. The annual report will be presented at the meeting.
   The annual report is to be presented at the meeting.

Exercise 4 Seite 8

1. Einstein und Da Vinci werden als Genies angesehen.
2. Man sagt, er sei eine sehr seltsame Person.
3. Man meint, sie sei faul und unzuverlässig.
4. Es wird allgemein geglaubt, dass seine Eltern extrem reich sind.
5. Du sollst charmant, gutaussehend und sehr witzig sein.

Exercise 5 Seite 8

1. simple present	am/is/are	+ past participle
2. present progressive	am/is/are being	+ past participle
3. simple past	was/were	+ past participle
4. past progressive	was/were being	+ past participle

5. present perfect — has/have been + past participle
6. past perfect — had been + past participle
7. will-future — will be + past participle
8. going to-future — am/is/are going to be + past participle

Exercise 6 Seite 9

1. I have been offered a better job by a rival firm.
   A better job has been offered to me by a rival firm.
2. We were served coffee and biscuits by the boss's secretary.
   Coffee and biscuits were served to us by the boss's secretary.
3. My mother was given an award for her work with a local charity.
   An award was given to my mother for her work with a local charity.
4. We were shown photos of criminals.
   Photos of criminals were shown to us.
5. My grandparents in Minsk were sent an e-mail with some photos.
   An e-mail with some photos was sent to my grandparents in Minsk.
6. I was offered a lift into town by my sister.
   A lift into town was offered to me by my sister.
7. All Mrs Brown's pupils were given a small prize.
   A small prize was given to all Mrs Brown's pupils.
8. Our guests were shown a video film of our last holiday.
   A video film of our last holiday was shown to our guests.
9. Our grandmother was sent flowers.
   Flowers were sent to our grandmother.

1.2 *Conditional sentences*

Exercise 1 Seite 10

1D, 2G, 3A, 4H, 5B, 6C, 7F, 8E

Exercise 2 Seite 10

B. We can have a barbecue if the weather is good.
C. I won't take your photo if you don't smile.
D. We must leave now if we want to arrive on time.
E. Bob will be in the semi-finals if he wins this game.
F. Will you pay me £2 if I wash and polish the car?
G. I'll bring my new CDs if Liz brings her CD player.
H. We'll stay at home and watch a film if the weather is bad.

Exercise 3 Seite 11

1D, 2G, 3B, 4E, 5A, 6H, 7F, 8C

Exercise 4 Seite 11

(Die Alternativen in Klammern sind auch möglich.)

1. I'*ll answer* these letters today if I *have* time.
   (*I'm going to* answer these ...)
2. If we *leave* now, we *won't be* late.
3. Tom *will buy* a newspaper if he *remembers*.
4. *Will you* help me if I *ask* nicely?
5. I'*m going to* have a long rest if I get the chance.
   (I'*ll have* a long rest ...)
6. I *won't* disturb you if you'*re working*.
   (I'*m* not *going to* disturb you ...)
7. I'*ll wash* up if you'*ll dry* the dishes.
   (I'*ll wash* up if you *dry* the dishes.)

Exercise 5 Seite 11

1. If we *went* to New York, we *could admire* the view from the observation platform at the top of the Empire State Building.
2. If you *had* a sense of humour, you *wouldn't take* yourself so seriously.
3. If you *weren't* so insensitive, you *would understand* my feelings better.
4. If Jane *didn't help* me with my Maths homework, I *wouldn't be able to* keep up in class.
5. If he *explained* things more clearly, his pupils *wouldn't ask* so many questions.
6. If Tom and Rick *were* more careful workers, their boss *wouldn't complain* so much.
7. If Lucy *didn't lie* so much, people *would like* her a lot better.
8. If we *found* the missing piece, we *could complete* this jigsaw puzzle!
9. If people *knew* what went into these sausages, they *wouldn't eat* them.

Exercise 6 Seite 12

Lösungsvorschlag:

1. If I were a rabbit, I would love carrots.
2. If I were a crocodile, I would be very lazy.
3. If I were Batman, I could rescue the whole world.
4. If I were Robin Hood, everyone would admire me.
5. If I were a billionaire, I could buy everything I wanted.
6. If I were on holiday, I wouldn't have to go to school today.
7. If you enjoyed the party so much, why did you leave so early?

Exercise 7 Seite 13

1. I *would have won* the race if I *hadn't fallen over*.
2. If I *had gone* out, I *might have missed* Isabel's call.
3. If Susan *had bought* those shoes, she *would have regretted* it.
4. I *wouldn't have lost* all my money if I *hadn't betted* on that horse!
5. If I *hadn't jumped* out of the way, I *would now be* dead!
6. If I *hadn't bought* some food, we *would have had* nothing to eat.
7. If you *had asked* Mr Shepherd, he *would have helped* you.
8. If you *had answered* the question correctly, you *would have won* a million dollars.
9. If I *had prepared* for the interview, I *might have got* the job.
10. If Alice *had played* better, she *could have won*.
11. If Blue Lightning *had won* the race, he *would have made* lots of people very happy!

1.3 *Modal auxiliaries*

Exercise 1 Seite 14

1. can, 2. can/may, 3. May ...? (May ...? ist höflicher als Can ...?), 4. will ('ll), 5. can/may/might, 6. must/will, 7. must, 8. can, 9. can/may/might, 10. mustn't, 11. should, 12. needn't, 13. should, 14. mustn't, 15. will, 16. needn't

Exercise 2 Seite 15

1 a) I have to wait 5 minutes because the train is late.
1 b) I've got to wait 5 minutes because the train is late.
2 a) I don't have to get up early tomorrow, because I'm on holiday.
2 b) I haven't got to get up early tomorrow, because I'm on holiday.
3 a) My girlfriend tells me what I have to do.
3 b) My girlfriend tells me what I've got to do.

Exercise 3 Seite 16

1. mustn't, 2. can't, 3. could, 4. must, 5. can, 6. needn't, 7. can, 8. couldn't, 9. must, 10. mustn't, 11. needn't

Test

Exercise 1 Seite 17

1. were being shown, was described
2. were taken, was built, have just been made, was pulled down
3. were led, were informed, can/could now be seen, was not included, Has/Had the collection been sold
4. could/were to be found, be taken to, were stared at, had been placed, had been painted, were (being) herded, was/had been shot

Exercise 2 Seite 18

1. Type 2, 2. Type 1, 3. Type 2, 4. Type 1, 5. Type 1, 6. Type 3, 7. Type 3, 8. Type 2, 9. Type 1

Exercise 3 Seite 18

1. Diana *likes* science fiction ... 2. If I *saved* enough money, ... 3. If I *were* you, ... 4. If you *wanted* the blue blouse, ...? 5. If you *had asked* me nicely, ... 6. If you *paid* me £5, ... 7. If more cyclists *wore* something bright at night ... 8. If the cyclist *had been wearing* something bright, ... 9. If it *is* on a plate in front of him, ... 10. If we *hadn't moved,* ... 11. If you *knew* the correct answer, ...? 12. If he *needs* more money, ...

Exercise 4 Seite 18

1. We weren't able to (were unable to) go fishing yesterday because the weather was too rough.
2. If you have a bad toothache, you have to/have got to/will have to see a dentist.
3. Sarah was already able to ride a pony when she was seven.
4. Slow down, there's a school ahead and you aren't/you're not allowed to go faster than 20 mph.
5. You won't/don't have to stay at school next year if you get an apprenticeship.
6. Am I allowed to let my dog off the lead in this park?
7. The sign says that after 9 a.m. drivers have to pay $2 an hour to park here.
8. Is anybody here able to explain Einstein's general theory of relativity?
9. The concert doesn't start for another hour, so we don't have to hurry.
10. Some whales are able to dive to depths of 1500 metres and more.
11. Are we allowed to smoke in this part of the restaurant?

Exercise 5 Seite 19

1. needn't, 2. couldn't, 3. must, 4. might/could, 5. may/will, 6. Shall oder can/could, 7. can, 8. mustn't/shouldn't, 9. Would, 10. should/must

1.4 *The past tenses*

Exercise 1 Seite 20

1C, 2C, 3D, 4A, 5F, 6E, 7A, 8A, 9B, 10A, 11B, 12A

Exercise 2 Seite 20

1. was backing out of – ran into, 2. wasn't looking, 3. took, 4. has been working, 5. has replaced

Exercise 3 Seite 21

1. were feeling – arrived, 2. was sitting – reading – started, 3. were driving – slowing down – happened, 4. woke up – was – was running – dripping, 5. knew – was walking – went, 6. arrived – were eating – having – watching, 7. was cutting, broke down

Exercise 4 Seite 22

1. My Grandma has never driven a car. 2. Have you ever seen the Golden Temple in Amritsar? 3. Did you visit Rome when you were in Italy last summer? 4. I have lost my car key somewhere. 5. Have you ever had a tetanus injection? 6. When did you have your last tetanus injection? 7. Have you found your coat yet? 8. Where did you find your coat?

Exercise 5 Seite 22

1. Have you talked 2. had – told, 3. hasn't attended – have never been, 4. discussed – sent, 5. have just read, 6. gave – Have you had, 7. (has) crashed – hasn't been able to

Exercise 6 Seite 23

1. has been working, 2. have been promising, 3. has been reading, 4. has been dreaming, 5. has been stealing, 6. have been avoiding

Exercise 7 Seite 23

1. has called, 2. Has he left, 3. has given, 4. Have you been trying, 5. I've been phoning – Where have you been?, 6. I've spent – I've been visiting, 7. Haven't you heard, 8. What has happened?, 9. has just bought – has seen – has already left – has been interviewing

Exercise 8 Seite 24

1. have often visited/often visit – have been taking – have toured – had never stayed
2. spent – didn't just stay
3. chose – hired – drove – stopped – were looking for
4. had both retired– had sold – had been living – didn't want to – was
5. bought – have now extended/are now extending – modernized/modernizing

1.5 *The future tenses*

Exercise 1 Seite 25

1. D., 2. A., 3. E., 4. F., 5. B., 6. C.

Exercise 2 Seite 25

1. If, 2. when/as soon as, 3. when/as soon as, 4. if, 5. unless, 6. when/as soon as, 7. unless, 8. if, 9. when

Exercise 3 Seite 26

1. This is your schedule for the next three days Ms Chapman.
2. Your train arrives at King's Cross Station in London at 6.25 a.m.
3. Your flight isn't until 8.50.
4. That gives you enough time for a quick breakfast and the journey to Heathrow Airport.
5. Your plane makes a short stop in New York and then flies on to Orlando.
6. You pick up your car at the Ajax desk, drive to St Petersburg and check into the Marryat Hotel.
7. There's a road map in the glove compartment.
8. Your first meeting is next morning at 10.30.
9. Here's the address.
10. Your next meeting isn't until 6.30 p.m., so you've got plenty of time.

Exercise 4 Seite 26

Buckingham Palace – London – London

Exercise 5 Seite 27

Times	Places	Activities
9.15 a.m.	pick up outside hotel	go on sightseeing tour
10 a.m.	stop at Trafalgar Square	walk around, take photos
11 a.m.	stop at Buckingham Palace	walk around, take photos
12 p.m.	arrive Camden Lock	leave coach, street market
1 p.m.	World's End pub	have lunch
3 p.m.	canal	walk
5 p.m.	canal boat	have a disco party
8 p.m.	Pie Shop in Camden High Street	have traditional British supper
9.30 p.m.	underground station	travel back to hotel

Exercise 6 Seite 28

Lösungsvorschlag:

1. I'll give, 2. is going to give, 3. I'll show, 4. I'll turn, 5. I'm going to turn, 6. Will you help, 7. Are you going to do, 8. I'll bring back, 9. He's going to buy, 10. I'll call, 11. I'm going to call

Exercise 7 Seite 29

Lösungsvorschlag:

1. That boy is going to fall off his bike! (= unmittelbar)
2. Be careful or you'll hurt yourself! (= allgemeine Voraussage)
3. It'll be dark in an hour. (= allgemeine Voraussage)
4. I'm sure (that) Tom will be there. (= Vermutung usw.)
5. It'll snow tomorrow. (= allgemeine Voraussage)/It's going to snow tomorrow. (= Man denkt an die Anzeichen, die dafür sprechen.)
6. We'll be very busy tomorrow. (= allgemeine Voraussage)/We're going to be very busy tomorrow. (= Man denkt an die Gründe.)
7. I'm hungry. I'm going to make myself a sandwich. (=schon gefasste Absicht)
8. Jane is going to buy the food for our party. (=schon gefasste Absicht)
9. We'll stop at the next filling station. (= spontane Entscheidung)/We're going to stop at the next filling station. (= schon gefasste Absicht)
10. I promise I won't do it again. (= Vermutung usw.)

Exercise 8 Seite 30

1. I wonder if it will (still) be raining this time tomorrow?
2. Will you be playing tennis this afternoon?
3. Where will we/the team be playing next Sunday?
4. I'll be staying in/at home this evening.
5. Please come half an hour later because at 5.30 I'll (still) be doing my homework.
6. When will you be coming/arriving?
7. What will you be wearing (this evening)?
8. I'll be waiting outside the cinema.
9. I'll be travelling/going with three friends.

Exercise 9 Seite 30

1. will have done, 2. will have caught, 3. will have heard, 4. will have sold, 5. won't have started, 6. won't have arrived, 7. won't have spoken

1.6 *Reported speech*

Exercise 1 Seite 32

1. Bill said he didn't want to visit any museums that weekend.
2. Chris told us (that) she had been sleeping when the fire started.
3. Joe suggested (that) we should ride our bikes to the beach after school the next/following day.
4. Mark explained (that) they had been very angry when they discovered that Ben had lied to them.
5. Carol asked George when it would be convenient for him to visit.
6. Mike told us (that) he was going to write some letters before he went out.

Exercise 2 Seite 32

1. Alex: My grandfather keeps rabbits in his garden shed.
2. Linda: I was ill yesterday, so I didn't go to work.
3. Keith: I haven't prepared for the test tomorrow.
4. Mr Noble: Business hasn't been very good this month.

Exercise 3 Seite 33

1. Jim asked Jane if she had been shopping.
2. She said she had and asked him to help her carry some bags from the car.
3. Jim wanted to know where he should take them.
4. Jane told him to put them on the counter.
5. (Then) Jim asked if he could help her put everything away.
6. She asked him if he knew where it all went.
7. (So) he answered that the tins went in the cupboard and everything else went in the fridge.
8. (Then) Jane asked him to leave it, because she had her own system and he would just get everything muddled up.

Exercise 4 Seite 33

1. Jessica asked if anybody was feeling hungry.
2. Paul said he was and asked if she had any sandwiches.
3. Jessica said she had BLT sandwiches and tuna fish sandwiches.
4. Paul wanted to know what a BLT sandwich was.
5. Jessica told him it was a sandwich with bacon, lettuce and tomato and asked if he wanted one.

Test

Exercise 1 Seite 34

1J, 2H, 3Q, 4C, 5M, 6A, 7T, 8R, 9F, 10O, 11P, 12I, 13L, 14B, 15N, 16U, 17D, 18V, 19S, 20K, 21G, 22E

Exercise 2 Seite 35

had been walking – found
had heard – (had) left
had been making – cut – had flown off – revealed – had been eating
had once been
waved – held – examined
had turned away – (had) been/was being
had taken off – was talking
haven't been able to
moved – was trying
did – have been watching – entered
knew – were coming

had been searching
said – threw
caught – was

Exercise 3 Seite 35

Lösungsvorschlag:

1. Charles said he often took the dog for a walk in the park.
2. Ted explained that everybody had to have a ticket before they got on the train the following morning.
3. Tina said she was sorry, but she wouldn't be able to go on the class trip the following Friday.
4. Susan explained that she wasn't very hungry because she had eaten a big meal only an hour before.
5. Ian told us he had tried to talk to Alan the day before, but he hadn't listened (to him).

Exercise 4 Seite 36

1. Mrs Fox told her daughter to take her little brother to the beach with her and her friends.
2. Mr Oliver told his children to go with him. He wanted a word with both of them.
3. Susan asked her friend to help her clear the table and wash up.
4. Ms Thomson asked the boy why he hadn't told her that before.
5. Mark warned Sheila to open the box carefully or the hamster would escape.
6. The dentist asked the nurse how many people were waiting outside.
7. Mrs Wood reminded Mr Wood not to forget his coat when they left the restaurant.
8. Mr Watson asked Ms Wood to take the letters to the post office on her way home.
9. The waitress asked the Woods if they had enjoyed their meal.

Exercise 5 Seite 36

Lösungsvorschlag:

1. Mrs Fox asked her husband where that morning's newspaper was and if he had seen it.
2. He told her he was reading it and that he would be finished soon.
3. She asked him if he had read the part with the TV programmes.
4. (Then) he asked her if they were going out that evening.
5. She told him she didn't want to go out, (because) there was a good film on TV.
6. He asked her what the name of the film was and if he knew it.
7. She told him it was a love story and he wouldn't like it.
8. (So) Mr Fox agreed she should stay in and watch the film.
9. She asked her husband what he would be doing, and if he was going/intended to go to the pub.

1.7 *Infinitive and gerund constructions*

Exercise 1 Seite 37

1. The bad weather made us drive much more slowly.
2. Today we let our two sons cook a meal.
3. It's too late for the bus, we'd better call a taxi.
4. We'd rather visit the zoo than the museum.
5. We do hope you'll visit us again.
6. I helped Carla wash up after the meal.

Exercise 2 Seite 38

1. was having – heard – knock/knocking, 2. got out – went – looked, 3. saw – put/putting, 4. looked – noticed – make/making, 5. stopped, 6 saw – point, 7. got – walked, 8. heard – ring opened, 9. watched – open/opening, 10. realized – was not wearing, 11. felt – turn/turning

Exercise 3 Seite 39

1 E, 2 G, 3 B, 4 H, 5 A, 6 C, 7 F, 8 D

Exercise 4 Seite 39

1. I stopped at the kiosk to buy a newspaper.
2. He stopped breathing.
3. Ted tried hard to win the game.
4. I tried talking to him but it didn't work.
5. She remembered seeing a man.
6. She remembered to take her umbrella.
7. We've forgotten to buy bread.
8. She's already forgotten talking to us.

Exercise 5 Seite 39

1. to finish, 2, to see, 3. to read, 4. to get to, 5. to play, 6. to drive, 7. to wear, 8. to use, 9. to learn, 10. to know, 11. to like, 12. to lean, 13. to stop, 14. to make

Exercise 6 Seite 40

1. Miss Hardy was the only person from the office to congratulate me on my promotion.
2. I went into the house to see if everything was all right.
3. Armstrong was the first man to walk on the moon.
4. If you enjoy horror films, "Glibberspawn" is a film to watch.
5. I thought you would be the last person to help me.
6. I don't know anybody to talk to.
7. Children need people to look up to.

1.8 *Participles*

Exercise 1 Seite 41

1. excited, 2. exciting, 3. jumping, 4. stolen, 5. sleeping, 6. flying, 7. hidden, 8. fascinating, 9. fascinated, 10. used, 11. borrowed, 12. grinning, 13. loving, 14. freezing, 15. Frozen

Exercise 2 Seite 42

1. held up – tempting, 2. made – sent – isolated, 3. searching, 4. used – frightening, 5. worn, 6. found – stolen, 7. reported, 8. masked – seen – hidden, 9. sent – stopped, 10. dressed, 11. taken

Exercise 3 Seite 43

1. Before going to bed, we ..., 2. When using a grinder, you ..., 3. Although buried under three metres of snow, the skier ..., 4. If taken too often, this drug ..., 5. I always examine a car carefully before buying it. 6. Before starting a long journey, I ..., 7. Although defeated in the election, the president ..., 8. If asked politely, most people ...

Exercise 4 Seite 44

1. Seeing, 2. Grabbing, 3. Running, 4. Standing, 5. Noticing – picking up, 6. Shouting – throwing, 7. Looking – seeing, 8. Holding, 9. Laughing – cheering, 10. Noticing – pointing at

1.9 *Articles and nouns*

Exercise 1 Seite 45

1. a, 2. an, 3. a, 4. an, 5. an, 6. an, 7. an, 8. a, 9. an, 10. an, 11. an, 12. a, 13. a, 14. a, 15. a, 16. a, 17. a, 18. an, 19. an, 20. a

Exercise 2 Seite 45

a shopkeeper, Asians, a general store, the one, the street, an early morning walk, a son, an army camp, A large part, the British army, Germany, The Whittakers, the one daughter (or: one daughter), a waitress, a restaurant, a port, the north, The Taylors, an old couple, the Whittakers, the people, pensioners

Exercise 3 Seite 46

1. Tom Nash, June, New York, a Thursday, the week, Thanksgiving, Fred's Diner, a nice traditional ..., Macy's, Fifth Avenue, the end, a Mr Piper, Tom, Mr Piper, a Bill (or: Bill), Central Park, an hour, the waiting room, Grand Central Station, Mr Piper

Exercise 4 Seite 47

1. slice/packet/piece/pound, 2. slice/packet/pound, 3. jar, 4. can/bottle/barrel/litre, 5. can/carton/bottle/jug/litre, 6. packet/pound, 7. slice/piece, 8. bar/pound/piece

Exercise 5 Seite 47

1. E: fish(es), 2. H: birds, 3. J: ants, 4. A: monkeys, 5. G: bees, 6. B: flies, 7. D: lions, 8. C: dolphins, 9. F: puppies, 10. I: wolves

Exercise 6 Seite 48

1. J, 2. M, 3. E, 4. O, 5. B, 6. L, 7. A, 8. K, 9. C, 10. N, 11. F, 12. G, 13. H, 14. D

Test

Exercise 1 Seite 49

1. crawl/crawling, 2. to buy, 3. need, 4. to check, 5. to dance/dancing, 6. go/going, 7. to give, 8. to do, 9. get up/to get up, 10. burying, 11. to get, 12. get up - to stay, 13. to go - getting up, 14. examine, 15. to listen to, 16. stop - to check, 17. to tell/telling, 18. to sing/singing, 19. to get, 20. to swim, 21. play/playing, 22. to see, 23. to buy, 24. to take, 25. buying, 26. burning, 27. to apologise, 28. to serve

Exercise 2 Seite 50

1. After finishing our meal, ..., 2. Mrs Quinn is the woman selling ..., 3. The men caught by the police ..., 4. After watching the film, ..., 5. Is this the football used ...?, 6. Being very tired, ..., 7. I had an accident walking home. 8. After eating a big meal ..., 9. Seeing the fire, ..., 10. So this is the famous painting stolen ..., 11. Watching the tiger, ..., 12. Looking out of the window, ..., 13. Any idiot can do it if correctly trained. 14. When given everything they want, people ..., 15. (If) stewed slowly in red wine, ...

Exercise 3 Seite 50

1. were, 2. is, 3. doesn't, 4. are, 5. are, 6. goes, 7. are, 8. are, 9. Are, 10. is

1.10 *Conjunctions and prepositions*

Exercise 1 Seite 51

1. E, 2. G, 3. F, 4. B, 5. A, 6. H, 7. D, 8. C

Exercise 2 Seite 52

1. but - before, 2. Although, 3. because, 4. after/because - that, 5. so that

Exercise 3 Seite 52

1. Mr Smith has got a bad temper, and so has his wife. 2. I'm frightened of dogs, and so is my sister. 3. I can't stand rap music, and neither (nor) can my friends. 4. Jane hates science-fiction stories, and so do I. 5. Andy doesn't like Jeremy Warton, and nor (neither) do I. 6. Mr Digby never smiles, and neither (nor) does his wife. 7. Sunderland will never beat Manchester United, and neither (nor) will Middlesborough.

Exercise 4 Seite 53

1. and, 2. Both - and - but, 3. as well as, 4. As/Because, 5. after, 6. because/as, 7. because of, 8. unless, 9. even if

Exercise 5 Seite 53

in March, on a Friday, on the Saturday, at her parents' house, in Fox Terrace, in the afternoon, at home, at the supermarket, in Redcar Road, in the car park, on Saturdays, at the corner, at 7.30

Exercise 6 Seite 54

1. after, 2. during, 3. for, 4. by, 5. since, 6. before, 7. from ... to, 8. till/until, 9. till/until

Exercise 7 Seite 55

1. against, 2. among, 3. near, 4. around, 5. outside, 6. behind, 7. over/above

Exercise 8 Seite 55

1. I walked across the street. 2. I ran after the bus. 3. I walked down/along the street. 4. I walked through the park. 5. I looked out of the window. 6. I walked towards him. 7. I went into his office. 8. I walked past him. 9. Tom was angry and walked.

Exercise 9 Seite 56

1. über, 2. als, 3. von, 4. außer, 5. für, 6. zum Mittagessen, 7. statt, 8. von, 9. wie, 10. über, 11. mit, 12. ohne

Exercise 10 Seite 56

1. grow up, 2. cut down, 3. cut off, 4. cut out, 5. agree with, 6. show off, 7. ask for, 8. give up, 9. drop out, 10. break in, 11. break out, 12. give away, 13. fall behind, 14. fall over, 15. climb up, 16. get off, 17. cheer up, 18. get up, 19. blow up, 20. set up, 21. fill in, 22. hand out, 23. aim at, 24. find out

1.11 *Translating* wollen, sollen, lassen

Exercise 1 Seite 57

1. want to, 2. would like, 3. wish to, 4. wouldn't, 5. would like

Exercise 2 Seite 58

1. should/ought to, 2. are we expected/supposed to, 3. Shall ...?, 4. is said to, 5. are said to, 6. shouldn't, 7. had better, 8. had better, 9. is supposed to, 10. are intended to, 11. are to be

Exercise 3 Seite 59

1. They left the car and continued on foot.
2. She wouldn't let/allow him to play with her toys.
3. He can't stop swearing.
4. Once a year we have the car serviced.
5. I went in and had my hair cut.
6. They made me pay for the broken vase.
7. She won't let us explain anything.
8. I had the hedge cut.
9. He made us wait for hours.
10. Don't let the dog (come) in.

Test

Exercise 1 Seite 60

1. thieves, 2. chimneys, 3. sheep, 4. breadknives, 5. forget-me-nots, 6. wolves, 7. fish/fishes, 8. chiefs, 9. teeth, 10. fishermen, 11. shopping bags, 12. flies

Exercise 2 Seite 60

1. U, 2. P, 3. U, 4. C, 5. U, 6. C, 7. P, 8. U, 9. C, 10. U, 11. C, 12. C, 13. C, 14. U, 15. P

Exercise 3 Seite 60

1. a loaf of bread, 2. a pair of trousers, 3. customs, 4. manners, 5. a pair of scissors, 6. a compass / pair of compasses, 7. an item of news, 8. a barrel of beer, 9. a bar of chocolate, 10. a box of chocolates

Exercise 4 Seite 61

1. My mother is a doctor. 2. She works in the hospital in Victoria Road. 3. My father is a sales assistant. 4. He works at the Asco supermarket in Cromwell Street.

Exercise 5 Seite 61

1. when, 2. until, 3. but, 4. or, 5. and, 6. because, 7. because of, 8. whenever, 9. if, 10. unless, 11. and neither, 12. and so, 13. as, 14. after, 15. Whenever, 16. as soon as, 17. until, 18. Before, 19. while, 20. when, 21. since, 22. although

Exercise 6 Seite 62

1. after, 2. during, 3. for, 4. since, 5. till/until, 6. between

Exercise 7 Seite 62

1. before, 2. above, 3. in front of, 4. down, 5. outside, 6. over, 7. without, 8. into

Exercise 8 Seite 62

1. on, 2. away, 3. out, 4. up

Exercise 9 Seite 62

1. May we go now? 2. I may have known him. 3. Shall I open a window? 4. He ought to be ashamed. 5. May I sit here? 6. That may be so, but it's still wrong. 7. You may be right. 8. You ought to talk to your parents about it.

Exercise 10 Seite 63

Across 4. spectacle (Schauspiel), 6. cloth (Tuch), 8. customs (Zoll), 9. scissors (Schere), 12. police (Polizei), 13. tweezers (Pinzette), 14. cattle (Vieh) 15. clothes (Kleidung)
Down 1. pains (Bemühung), 2. pain (Schmerz), 3. glasses (Brille), 4. sheep (Schaf), 5. salmon (Lachs), 7. manners (Benehmen), 10. trousers (Hose), 11. pliers (Zange)

2.1 Lesen und verstehen

Not Asian Enough

Exercise 1 Seite 65

word family	similarity to German	context
sticky facial disrespectful	aroma dessert	fluently frown pretend spit out

Exercise 3 Seite 67

1. a.
2. Because there were better opportunities and chances for Beini Shi in the United States.
3. a.
4. d.
5. a.
6. b.
7. He was angry, disapproving, not very happy.
8. father, mother, daughter, son
9. c.
10. b.
11. Yes: she writes that she liked her mother's more open American lifestyle.
12. b.

Failing Teachers

Exercise 1 Seite 69

word family	similarity to German	context
successful destructive noisy categorize	plague administrator urban (Latin, French) undisciplined	loathing thug require diligent

Exercise 3 Seite 71

1. a.
2. No: the text says that you'll find these noisy, chaotic classrooms in almost any of America's big cities, not just New York.
3. They hold parents, students, administrators and teachers responsible.
4. Examples: kids playing dice in the back of the classroom, listening to their Walkman, writing rap rhymes, rapping to girls, and also practicing gang signs
5. He does not see any success for his hard work, but still does not give up.
6. d.
7. hard working/diligent, generous, helpful
8. The teachers don't care.
9. They are scared, cannot learn, they don't want to be in that environment, so they give up.
10. d.

2.2 Hören und verstehen

The Museum of the American West

Exercise 1 Seite 72

1 D, 2 H, 3 I, 4 E, 5 F, 6 J, 7 A, 8 G, 9 C, 10 B, 11 K

The Lakeside Hotel

Exercise 2 Seite 74

1. in his office every day, 9.00-10.30 a.m. and 2-3.30 p.m. plus 6-8 p.m. on Tuesdays and Thursdays. On his mobile.
2. Breakfast: 7.30-11 a.m.; self-; Lakeview.
   Lunch: from 11.30 a.m.-2.30 p.m.; Fox Hill Restaurant.
   Dinner: 6.30-8.30 p.m.; Lakeview Lounge; (hotel's famous) fish dishes
3. bike
4. games; indoor swimming-pool. The sports facilities are free. You must bring your own towels for sauna and swimming pool.
5. Steamboat. £15 per person. The hotel's own pier. 9 p.m. to midnight.
6. card

Beamish North of England Open Air Museum

Exercise 1 Seite 75

What you need to ask	Answers/information
Ticket prices for school groups	
- pupils	£7.50
- teachers	free
Opening times	
Tuesday – Sunday	10 a.m. to 6 p.m.
Monday	closed
How to get there if there is a bus	
- where can you get on?	Newcastle, Eldon Place bus station; Low Fell
- how much is it?	£4.50 adults; £2 children and school students
Food and drink	
- special advice/rules for schools	should bring packed lunch
Activities – is there an activity about	☑ yes ☐ no
- the life of a pupil about 150 years ago?	☑ yes ☐ yes
- cooking like your great-grandparents?	☐ yes ☑ no
- life on a farm?	☐ yes ☑ no
- the life of a fishwife?	☑ yes ☐ no
- railways?	
- How much are the activities?	£35 per group
- When must you book the activities?	four weeks before visit
Contact	
- web address	www.beamish.org.uk
- e-mail address	mail@beamish.uk

Test

Exercise 1 Seite 76

1. Patrick's phone number is London 3095827.
2. Sarah has read an ad in the New York Times.
3. Patrick wants Sarah to start work in September.
4. c.
5. a.
6. b.

	true	false
7. Sarah must have a driving licence.	☐	☑
8. You can't get to Tracy and Linda's kindergarten by car.	☐	☑
9. Patrick is the only driver in the Anderson family.	☐	☑
10. The Anderson's house is only five years old.	☐	☑
11. Patrick works as a steel engineer.	☐	☑
12. Sarah will have her own bathroom.	☑	☐

13. The au-pair agency will look after Sarah's health insurance, visa, and work permit.
14. During her year in London, Sarah can go home at Christmas and Easter.
15. The Andersons will pay for Sarah's flights at the beginning of her stay, at the end of her stay and for one visit home.
16. The Andersons' last au-pair went home at Christmas and to the Continent at Easter.
17. Sarah wants to work from September to August because she wants to start university in September.
18. Sarah's reference number with Au-Pair-World-Wide is SW – 1209 – BMX – US.
19. Sarah's e-mail address is S.W.daughter@aupair.com.
20. Patrick's e-mail address is Patrick@anderson.com.

3.1 Über erzählende Texte *(fiction)* schreiben

Can I Help You?

Exercise 2 Seite 81

Lösungsvorschlag:

The narrator, an assistant in a baker's shop, relates a typical encounter with a certain customer. She is not exactly fond of this rich lady and nor are the other assistants in the shop. She dislikes her outward appearance as much as the way she talks. The lady talks without pauses and is never content with the things the assistant gives her. The narrator concludes that her behaviour is typical of people from a higher social class.

Exercise 3 Seite 82

character's outward appearance
thin lips, white teeth, too white; pink, diseased, old-lady gums; unnatural smile; eyes too squinty and sparkling; day-old mascara clings; expensive pantsuit; smells of perfume and old money; silk shirt; frail shoulders; baubles; spider-fingers; saccharine stare; high heels clicking; stench of her perfume
her way of speaking
speaks rapidly, repeats the same phrases: "Hello dear how are you oh wonderful ..." "... be a dear, oh thank you dear."
her actions
taps against the glass counter; annoying fussiness; discontented and hard to please; orders the narrator around; exchanges all the goods
what she says
"... they are just to die for"; "... dear me, you're so thin if I worked here well I would never be able to these wonderful treats would all be too hard to resist ..." comments and value judgments; false impression of friendliness
what others say/do
... you saw her first, you deal with her; sighing

Exercise 4 Seite 83

Lösungsvorschlag:

The assistants in the shop do not really want to serve the lady ("you saw her first, you deal with her", ll. 10-11) and the narrator turns to her with a sigh. The narrator's dislike of the lady becomes clear in the choice of words when she describes her appearance and behaviour. She wears expensive clothes but her look seems overdone. Her teeth are "too white", her smile "unnatural" (ll. 1-3) and her eyes "too squinty and sparkling" with a "saccharine stare" (l. 13), on her fingers there are "baubles" (l. 6), not jewellery. All this gives her an artificial appearance. Expensive clothes, a silk shirt, a white pantsuit and high heels add to this impression. Moreover, the narrator uses a large number of negative words: "Thin lips" (l. 1), "pink, diseased old-lady gums" (l. 2), a smell of "perfume and old money" (l. 5), later even the "stench" (l. 31) of her perfume, "day-old mascara", which "clings" (l. 4) in the lady's eyes, "frail shoulders" and "spider-fingers" (l. 6) show the narrator's strong dislike of the lady's outward appearance. She taps against the glass bakery counter, which reveals her impatience and suggests that she is used to commanding. The way the lady speaks is annoying. She speaks rapidly, without pauses. She uses the word "dear" (l. 16) several times, interjections like "oh" (l. 17), and words like "wonderful" and "delicious" (ll. 18-19), which show that her language is as overdone as her appearance. In this context, even her compliments ("they are just to die for", ... "you are so thin" ...., "wonderful treats", ... "too hard to resist" (ll. 18-19)) seem to be false. She is never content with what the narrator offers her.

Exercise 5-6 Seite 83

no reason and compassion in higher classes	
pros	**cons**
variety of choice fussy high positions in their jobs, employ servants used to giving orders, comfortable lives out of touch	education → reason education → wide horizons → compassion manners, etiquette experience: many don't look or act rich

reason and compassion reserved for working class	
pros	**cons**
know the dark sides of life	often poorly educated (see above) experience: reckless behaviour in public, sometimes contempt for reason from lack of education

Exercise 7 Seite 84

Lösungsvorschlag:

It is more than understandable that the shop assistants dislike this rich customer. But is her behaviour to do with social class? One could argue that high class people are used to a large choice and excellent quality of goods. Thus they may be fussy about anything they choose to buy. They are also used to giving orders. They hold high positions in their jobs and they may employ servants at home. This may lead to arrogant behaviour toward people who serve them in shops or restaurants. As they live comfortable lives they may be out of touch with the majority of the population, who have to work hard to earn their living.

However, we cannot generalise. Rich people are often well educated and education has to do with reason and also compassion. Educated people should have learned to feel with other people. Educated people, people from higher classes, should also have learned good manners. And many of them have. They don't even look rich, they don't want to show off and they behave like you and me.

Furthermore, compassion and reason are certainly not qualities reserved to the working class. You will find many people of low social status, poorly educated people who don't care about their fellow human beings, although they know the dark sides of life. Anti-social behaviour like shouting, smoking, spitting and swearing in public is surely more common among less educated people. Very often these people will not listen to reasonable arguments; reason is often despised by them. But again, it is not possible to generalise.

Summing up, I definitely do not think that reason and compassion are a matter of social class. Society is more complex than that and one has to take a more differentiated view of it.

Exercise 8 Seite 85

original choice of words (appearance)	contrasting positive words	original choice of words (language)	contrasting positive words
thin lips, white teeth, too white; pink, diseased, old-lady gums; unnatural smile; eyes too squinty and sparkling; day-old mascara clings; expensive pantsuit smells of perfume and old money; silk shirt; frail shoulders; baubles; spider-fingers; saccharine stare; high heels clicking; stench of her perfume	clean teeth friendly smile twinkling eyes make-up nice clothes slim rings, jewels slender sweet look scent of perfume	speaks rapidly, repeats the same phrases: “Hello dear how are you oh wonderful ...” “... be a dear, oh thank you dear.”	very friendly
		annoying fussiness	exclusive tastes

Lösungsvorschlag:
She is my favourite customer. Always elegantly dressed. She is rather old, but still cares about her looks. She looks younger in her white pantsuit, a loose shirt makes her look more casual, silk though, cotton would make her look vulgar. She always wears make-up, pink lipstick and mascara, despite her age, and it perfectly matches the colours of her clothes. Her teeth are well looked after, not a spot of yellow, let alone decay or even a gap. So she gives you the friendliest smile when she enters the shop, together with a lively twinkle in her eyes. She walks in that cloud of perfume that makes old ladies so lovely. Her body is slim, her fingers slender, not a gram of fat. The rings on her fingers show her good taste.
Her wishes are always exclusive. She doesn't read what everybody reads. She doesn't take the books from the display. She is very thoughtful when it comes to choosing her books and she is not easily satisfied, which shows her distinctive taste. She is so sweet when she talks, always calling me “dear”. I wish more customers were like her.

The Wave

Exercise 2 Seite 88

Lösungsvorschlag:
This excerpt from *The Wave* tells how Laurie, the editor-in-chief of the school magazine, is bullied because of a critical article she has written.
After her work in the office of the school magazine late that day, Laurie is alone in the school building. She wants to leave a book in her locker. When she gets to her locker she sees that someone has written the word ‘enemy’ on the door. Then she thinks that somebody is following her. Frightened, she runs towards the exit and manages to escape.

Exercise 3-4 Seite 89

light	sounds	mood	other
dark, corridors darkened, dark hallway	silence, sounds she'd never heard before, hums, buzzes, bubbling, splashing, unusually loud hollow echo	alone, empty school, eerie	empty school, hard floor

Exercise 5 Seite 89

Lösungsvorschlag:

The narrator creates an eerie, spooky atmosphere. Laurie is alone in the empty school. It is dark outside, and inside the "corridors were darkened", and the hallway is dark, too. At first there is no sound, only "the silence of the empty school". But then there are "sounds she'd never heard before", strange sounds, like hums, buzzes, bubbling, splashing and the "unusually loud hollow echo" of her own footsteps. These sounds, and the hard corridor floor add to the eerie atmosphere. The atmosphere anticipates the events that follow.

Exercise 6 Seite 89

Key events:

1. echoing footsteps
2. Laurie froze; the word "enemy" was painted
3. sound of footsteps grew louder
4. lights went out
5. Laurie was running

climax: doors were locked
relief: miraculously they opened

Exercise 7 Seite 90

Lösungsvorschlag:

Laurie's fear begins to grow when she sees the word "enemy" on her locker (line 28). It increases when she hears footsteps and even more so when the footsteps grow louder (line 35). The next key event is in line 36, when the electric lights in the corridor go out.

The climax is reached in line 41 when Laurie tries to open the doors: they are locked. Finally the tension is relieved, when "miraculously" they open (line 42) and Laurie can breathe the "cool evening air" (line 43).

Exercise 8 Seite 91

Lösungsvorschlag:

Laurie is bullied for her different opinion, which she has stated in the school magazine. But every day, students are bullied for a number of other reasons, too. Bullying is a serious problem for a lot of young people. At my school there are a few students who are victims of bullying. For example, there is a boy who is different from the others because he is very intelligent and speaks in a way only grown-ups usually use. He knows a lot of words and uses them beautifully. His marks are always excellent.

Another example is a girl who is not exactly pretty. People make fun of her hair, her face and her weight.

The obvious reason why students are bullied is that they are different in some way. Peer pressure plays an important part in persuading the others to join in with the crowd.

The consequences are obvious: people who are bullied will be deeply hurt. They will suffer and then react in various ways. Aggression or suicide could be extreme reactions.

To my mind, teachers, parents and students should find ways to deal effectively with this problem. Students should stand up against peer pressure, teachers should offer help to the victims, and parents must encourage their children to respect others, so that our schools will be safe places for everybody.

Exercise 9 Seite 92

Lösungsvorschlag:

Dear Editors, dear Gordon High Students,
I'm writing to you because there have been incidents in our school that we can't accept. We have all heard about the new movement "The Wave", which a lot of students are fascinated by. Basically it is a good thing when students get together and get organized in order to follow a common goal. In this case, however, something seems to have gone wrong. There are cases of bullying in our school against students who don't want to be part of the movement. A critical article in this paper has even led to an attack against the author of the article. The word "enemy" was written on her locker and she herself has been intimidated. We can't accept that people are attacked for holding a different opinion from that of others, even if these are in the majority. This is against the basic ideals of our country. Freedom of speech is one of our most important values. If we allow journalists to be intimidated, it will be the end of the free press. So everybody, each one of us, should think twice about their support for a movement like that. Maybe it is not quite what it seems.
X. Y.

Test

Unterlegte Textstellen sind Aspekte, die inhaltlich erwartet werden. Die sprachliche Darstellungsleistung kann hier nicht beurteilt werden. Du kannst z. B. deine/n Lehrer/in bitten, deine Texte zu beurteilen (vgl. S. 107).

Exercise 2 Seite 94

Lösungsvorschlag:

The narrator and the boy are in the same class. As he seems to be rather shy at first, the boy never returns the girl's smile when he looks at her. Every day she looks at his blue eyes, which fascinate her. She also smiles at him every day but does not even know if he notices.
His behaviour changes one day. He comes into class, walks to her desk and sits next to her. After staring and smiling at her the whole lesson, he tells her how much he likes her eyes.

Exercise 3 Seite 94

Lösungsvorschlag:

Both students are outsiders in their class. The boy is the smartest boy in school and seems to be good-looking, but he appears to be very shy, hiding his "deep blue eyes" (l. 15) behind his "thick black hair" (l. 16). One of the dominant features the narrator repeats again and again is how he keeps his "head down" (l. 1), his "head lowers" (l. 5), even "to its limit", he "turns his head" (l. 7) to avoid the narrator's smile and he leaves "quickly" (l. 2) to avoid confrontation. He seems ashamed to be there.
The narrator calls herself an "outcast" (l. 10). Unlike the other girls, she doesn't like shopping or showing off. She sits by herself and "is the subject of gossip and cruelty" (l. 11).
At the end of the text, the boy's behaviour is described as the complete opposite. He comes into the room "his head high" (l. 21–22), walking slowly. Instead of avoiding eye contact he stares at the narrator and seeks communication ("he stands as I stand" (l. 25)). He returns the smile she gives him. His eyes are no longer hidden but "gleam" (l. 26) with a smile.

Exercise 4 Seite 94

Lösungsvorschlag:

The boy has apparently gained self-confidence by realizing the girl's interest in him. His intelligence and good looks have obviously not been sufficient to reduce his shyness. This shows how important it is to be accepted by a group. Some people may be loners and not care what other people think about them, but most people need the acceptance of their peers. Especially in school, being an outsider must be hard and cruel. Of course, there are students who ask for it. There are some who are aggressive, others who are arrogant or unpleasant. These people should try to think about themselves and change their habits. Others, however, are just bullied because they are different. They may be smarter, may have a different taste as far as clothes or music go, may be smaller, or not so good at sports, in sum: not so cool. When these students are bullied, one should stand up for them, show courage, not give in to the peer pressure exerted by those who think they are better. Talking to them, giving them a smile – just like in Misha H.'s story – may help a great deal.

Exercise 5 Seite 94

Lösungsvorschlag:

It's the same drag every morning. I hear them whisper about me, cracking jokes I'm supposed to hear. I walk quickly to my seat, don't look at them. I concentrate on my work. It's all so easy, really. The teachers present me as a model student. As if it was difficult. Anybody with brains could understand the stuff we have to do. But they all stare at me as if I was from a different planet. I hate that stare.
There's this girl, though. She also stares at me. Does she want to make fun of me? I avoid her, although I like her. She has gorgeous eyes. Why does she look at me? She even smiles at me. Yes, I realize she's smiling at me. Other people smile, too. But I know they don't mean it. Does she mean it? She isn't one of them, really. She's different from the other girls, doesn't think much of shopping or giggling. She's also an outsider. She means it. I'm sure she means it. I know.
So next morning I sit next to her. I walk up to her, upright. It takes some courage, but I look at her during the lesson. All the time. She likes it, smiling all the time. At the end of the lesson I tell her: "You have gorgeous green eyes". I wonder what will happen next ...

3.2 Über Sachtexte *(non-fiction)* schreiben

Energy drinks

Exercise 2 Seite 97

Just from looking at the headline, the photograph and the caption I think the article deals with *the dangers of caffeine or energy drinks when they are consumed by schoolchildren.*

Exercise 3 Seite 98

Headline	**schools warned**	**pupils hooked**	**energy drinks**			
Paragraph 1	children becoming dependent	concentration	behaviour	signs of agitation	excessive caffeine consumption	
Paragraph 2	new government measures					
Paragraph 3	growing problem	drug education programme	illegal drugs	legal highs		
Paragraph 4	way to school break lunchtime	drinks: up to 160 mg caffeine	tablets: 50 mg caffeine	combat tiredness	improve performance/ concentration	Bruzz particular problem
Paragraph 5	schools concerned	abuse of energy drinks	use at exam time			
Paragraph 6	marketed to help through exams	schools teaching addiction	average person	average lifestyle	no need for energy drinks	
Paragraph 7	Bruzz spokesman	children more sensitive to caffeine	don't recommend Bruzz to children			

Exercise 4 Seite 98

	Heading	lines
1	Caffeine-sensitive people should avoid caffeine	33–35
2	Pupils become dependent on energy drinks	1–5
3	Schools only know how to deal with illegal drugs	12–19
4	Energy drinks as helpers in times of exam pressure	29–32
5	Schools teach children to develop addiction	25–28
6	Government advising on school food	6–11
7	Tait warns on the when, where and what of energy drinks and caffeine tablets	20–24

Exercise 5 Seite 99

D	C	D	B	A	B	A	C

Exercise 6 Seite 99

positive aspects
combat tiredness improve performance boost concentration help pupils through exams
negative/critical aspects
abuse of energy drinks children becoming more and more dependent agitation as a result of excessive caffeine consumption danger of encouraging addiction

Zusammenfassung *(summary)*

Exercise 1 Seite 100

5

Exercise 2 Seite 101

The article "Schools warned of pupils hooked on energy drinks", by Polly Curtis, published in *The Guardian*, September 3, 2008, is about the dangers of energy drinks for schoolchildren.
The author points out that more and more schoolchildren are consuming caffeine. An anti-drugs advisory group has told schools that many schoolchildren are becoming dependent on caffeine, which has a negative effect on their school life. Schools often do not know what to do about the problem, because their anti-drug campaigns deal only with illegal drugs.
The author then shows how schoolchildren "get hooked" on caffeine: many start using energy drinks when they have their exams, because they think that the drinks and tablets will make them less tired and improve their concentration and performance. This is what advertisements for energy drinks are telling young students.

Analyse *(analysis)*

Exercise 1 Seite 102

word	level of interest				
	1	2	3	4	5
Schools			X		
warned of					X
pupils			X		
hooked on					X
energy drinks				X	

Exercise 2 Seite 102

category	number of occurrences
"dealing with a threat" or "giving a warning"	5
"increase" or "become more important/serious"	2
"drug abuse and addiction"	7

Exercise 3 Seite 102

3

Exercise 4 Seite 103

Expertenanteil: ca 50%
Das Zitieren von Expertenmeinungen verleiht den Aussagen des Textes und damit dem Artikel insgesamt eine höhere Autorität bzw. Glaubwürdigkeit. Dies ist in diesem Fall insbesondere daran erkennbar, dass die Experten sich alle in leitenden Positionen befinden bzw. nationale Bedeutung haben.

Der Experte von Bruzz hingegen ist „nur" ein Unternehmenssprecher, womit die argumentative Einseitigkeit des Artikels nochmals verdeutlicht wird.

Exercise 5 Seite 103

Anzahl der positiven Aspekte ohne kritische Ergänzung: 0

Anzahl der positiven Expertenmeinungen: 0

Lösungsvorschlag:

Die Häufigkeit der Ausdrücke, die mit Warnung zu tun haben, legt nahe, dass der Text eine moralische Botschaft verbreiten will. Die Autorin versucht durch die kommentierende Darstellung, die Meinung der Leserinnen und Leser zu beeinflussen. Die Tatsache, dass keine positiven Argumente ohne kritischen Kommentar bleiben und dass alle Expertenmeinungen in die gleiche Richtung zielen, zeigt, dass die Autorin überzeugen will. Ihre Argumente werden schließlich auch von der „energy drinks"-Firma Bruzz geteilt (Z. 33–35). Dies vermittelt den Eindruck der Abgeschlossenheit in der Argumentation: Die Art und Weise, wie die Argumente vorgebracht werden, zeigt, dass die Autorin davon ausgeht, in ihrem Text Recht zu haben.

Exercise 6 Seite 104

Lösungsvorschlag:

Working with expert opinion is an important feature of Polly Curtis' article. Almost half the article is made up of quotations from various experts. Polly Curtis names three persons in positions of authority, plus the Bruzz representative, who is merely a company spokesperson. Additionally the author mentions the government and uses the collective term "experts".

The main function of expert opinion in this article is to give greater authority to the information presented in the text. Through it the author increases the credibility of her message. What she states is not just her own opinion; it is supported by the comments of people who have been working with the problem for a long time.

While this holds true mainly for Bob Tait in his function as a member of a drug education advisory group, the roles of Malcolm Trobe and Margaret Morrissey are a bit different. As policy director of a national organization of head teachers, Malcolm Trobe is an authority and a decision-maker. As a headmaster himself, he is also faced with the problem at a day-to-day level. Margaret Morrissey's function is similar: she, too, is a person in authority, and she represents another national group concerned with education, the parents.

The Bruzz spokesman also represents a party involved in the issue. Although one would expect him to defend the industry's position, his rather weak comment is very much in line with what the other experts say, and thus he also supports Polly Curtis' argument.

So, while quoting experts or people concerned always helps to make an article more interesting to the readers, Polly Curtis' use of these quotations mainly serves to make the reader agree with her message: beware of the dangers of possible caffeine-addiction for (your) children.

Stellungnahme *(comment)*

Exercise 1 Seite 104

Lösungsvorschlag:

(Argument 1)

To begin with, I'd like to state that a successful school career is probably the most important goal in any pupil's life. If you don't get good grades in your final exams, the choices of what you will be able to do in life will decrease considerably. At least, you will find it much more difficult to find a job that's interesting, challenging, secure – and well-paid. So it's not surprising that a pupil might try everything to get these top results, no matter what is involved in getting them.

(Argument 2)

Secondly, if a pupil tries to increase his or her chances to get better exam results by using stimulants like energy drinks, he or she has every right to do so. The drinks are sold legally, and if they can help you to perform better in an exam, or help you to put in that extra hour of revision or preparation, there seems to be no reason not to use them. This is not a sports competition, where the idea of fair play is central. In fact, this is about personal competition for your best chances in your future life.

(Argument 3)

So, while in sports part of the excitement comes from the fact that everybody relies on their physical and mental abilities, and doping means nothing but cheating, helping your body with stimulating energy drinks or pills isn't cheating on any spectator or getting an advantage over an opponent, but simply optimizing your own abilities - especially as these substances are not illegal.

(Argument 4)

Furthermore, the substance used is not only legal, it is also one of the most-widely used stimulant substances in the world - you can't really imagine a breakfast without tea or coffee.

So, in a society where personal success seems to matter most, trying to do better by helping your body and brain to perform better when it matters just can't be wrong.

(Argument 5)

However, a lot of people like doctors and teachers keep complaining. *One must take into consideration that* the problem seems to lie with the long-term effects, and/or side effects, of using stimulating drinks or pills from an early age. The side effects of caffeine consumption observed by teachers and doctors seem to outweigh the positive effects that pupils who consume energy drinks or take caffeine pills are hoping for.

Although caffeine may help you to stay awake longer to do your homework or revise, it may make you less able to concentrate where it really matters, in class. If you can't concentrate when the teacher explains the new material, and you have difficulty understanding the lesson, you will find it even harder to revise, because you haven't got the basic knowledge to start from.

(Argument 6)

Besides, this situation may easily be the beginning of a development which, like a vicious circle, will spiral off into something as serious as addiction to caffeine, especially as younger children seem to be much more sensitive to the effects of caffeine than adults.

So, although this drug is legal, it is still a drug and therefore contains all the risks of drug-taking: it can turn into a habit, it can become an addiction, and if you need more and more caffeine to achieve the effect you want, your body and mind will react vehemently when you try to get off the drug.

Therefore it must be clearly stated that, tempting as these substances are made to appear through the marketing departments of their manufacturers, using them means you are taking an extremely high risk of achieving just the opposite of what you aim for. And in that case you will be the long-term loser, because you have ruined your body for short-term success.

(Argument 7)

Taking into consideration that exams are basically designed so that the average pupil can pass them, there should really be no need for the use of stimulants. Just working normally and continuously, doing homework regularly, not allowing yourself too much time off, may work out much better in the long run than the short-lived blasts of caffeine-supported power-revising.

(Argument 8)

Perhaps the most important point is that when you know that your results are all your own work, that you have achieved them without this little extra help from a drug, you will feel all the better for it, because you have achieved something that you can really be proud of. This, in turn, will most likely help you to succeed in similar situations later in your life, because you know that you have got it in you to face even difficult challenges and with this degree of self-confidence that's based on real abilities you will gain a real advantage over your competitors.

(Conclusion)

Considering these points, I think there can only be one answer to the question whether pupils should use caffeine to boost their school success, and this answer is definitely "No, they should not", especially because the risks of long-term damage far outweigh any possible short-term benefits from improved exam performance. *I, personally*, would never rely on this external help, nor would I recommend its use to anyone at school, no matter how hard the exam pressure might seem to be.

Kreative Schreibaufgabe *(creative task)*

Exercise 1 Seite 107

Lösungsvorschlag:

5, Hawthorne Lane
East Boldon NE 36 3DP

14th June, 2012

Wendy Woodland
Youth Issues
Newcastle upon Tyne NE 25 6AW

Dear Wendy,

I am thirteen years old and I go to school here in Boldon. I am not doing too badly at school. Life at school used to be OK, but lately it has become more and more difficult. The problem is that I've got a friend in my class, John, who has gone completely crazy. He doesn't talk about anything except school exams, like how hard they are and how important it is to do well, and how coming second is not good enough and that you can't waste a minute of revision time, because you don't want to blame yourself for being lazy and being a failure. He's really wound up. He doesn't come to football practice during the week any more, although he used to love the game. He won't even come out at the weekends, not even for a short walk, let alone to watch a couple of DVDs with me.
On top of this, he looks terrible. He is extremely pale and his eyes are hollow and red. In class he can't sit still (which I don't mind, but the teachers do, so he gets into trouble all the time) and he just doesn't listen (I do mind that, because he never listens to me, either). When I ask him if there's anything wrong with him, he becomes very aggressive - it seems as if he just can't relax at all.
Last Tuesday his hand was even shaking when he was sitting at his desk waiting for the beginning of the next lesson. What I noticed is that he seems to get through a lot of energy drinks, four or five cans a day easily - and that's just during school hours. He hangs around the school cafeteria, too, trying to get older students to buy coffee for him - because the cafeteria staff won't serve younger pupils anything containing caffeine.
Would you say that my friend is a caffeine addict? Is that really possible, I mean, at his age? He isn't even fifteen yet. Please tell me what I ought to do. Should I confront him with the problem directly? Should I get in touch with his parents - or would that ruin our friendship? I'm really worried about John, so please write back soon.
Looking forward to your good advice

Yours
Patrick Derwent

Test

Unterlegte Textstellen sind Aspekte, die inhaltlich bewertet werden. Die sprachliche Darstellungsleistung kann hier nicht beurteilt werden. Du kannst z. B. deine/n Lehrer/in darum bitten.

Exercise 1 Seite 110

Lösungsvorschläge:

In his article, "Why we should step in to halt bad behaviour", published in *The Guardian,* September 3, 2008, Michael Hann lists arguments for and against active intervention in case of anti-social behaviour.
Using the voice of his wife to put the case against getting involved, the author argues that this may result in physical assault, possibly with fatal consequences, and questions its effectiveness, making the point that intervention may be seen as provocative and so in the long run be socially counterproductive. Furthermore, he points out that getting involved normally induces anger, which often results in high blood pressure or similar stress-related symptoms. Finally, he observes that the case for intervention may be seen as originating in an obsession for law and order and a right-wing political attitude.
However, there are strong reasons for getting involved, too. Anti-social behaviour reduces the quality of life for the entire society we live in and therefore it is the responsibility of every member of society to fight against it. This responsibility cannot simply be delegated to the police. Whereas the British seem to be developing a bystander mentality, other European countries show that active social responsibility is not incompatible

with a modern western society. Furthermore, the argument that intervention increases violence and danger is questionable, as (at least in London) the number of knife attacks has dropped in recent years. Finally the author points out that getting involved is an originally left-wing attitude, one that comes from the belief that society only functions if everybody is prepared to actively take responsibility.

Exercise 2 Seite 110

The author uses typical journalistic methods to convince the reader of his point of view, setting up a system of pros and cons and going on to list the counter-arguments before singling out one of these – the impact of anger on blood pressure and general health – as a springboard for his own position in favour of intervention. Each counter-argument – e.g. the danger and long-term ineffectiveness of intervention – is then opposed and refuted in turn. Expert opinion – e.g the think tank *Reform* – is included to lend weight to his arguments.
The author attracts the attention and sympathy of his readers by addressing them directly, citing personal experiences and asking "... shouldn't more people intervene? ... isn't the well-being of society the responsibility of the whole of society?" The use of the first person plural in the headline ("Why we should step in to halt bad behaviour") and at several points throughout the article has the same effect.
Finally Michael Hann clearly takes into consideration the political orientation of the *Guardian* as a newspaper supporting left-wing values. He defends his position against the accusation of being right-wing by integrating a quotation from the former British prime minister Margaret Thatcher, who said that there was no such thing as society. In doing so he lays responsibility for the development of an 'I-won't-get-involved' type of society at the doorstep of the former Conservative government. Getting involved, he argues, is a core Labour principle and the exact opposite of a call for a totalitarian police state. Hann's provocative, confrontational argument is typical of a newspaper journalist who is sure of the political and social sympathy of his readership.

Exercise 3 Seite 110

a)
I cannot definitely tell what my personal reaction might be in that sort of situation. I think most of us would say, if they were asked, that they would intervene in some way. But that's theory and you can't compare it to the real thing. Depending on the situation, although I might feel that I should confront the aggressor, I would probably be too scared of being attacked myself to intervene.
I guess many of us are afraid of the consequences of showing too much responsibility. In the example given in the task, there might well be a number of witnesses of the attack – other people I could call on to help. But I'm not sure if that would help me to act responsibly or hinder me from doing so. Many of us might be too shy to act in front of unknown people. Won't I look weird if I speak up? I don't want the others to have that impression ...
But sometimes you just need someone to give a starting signal, then the other passengers will assist you if you try to stop the aggressor. You have to have courage, that's clear – courage to take a risk. But if you don't, won't you feel bad that you have missed the chance to help another person who really needed it?
Generally, there should be no excuse for not helping. I mean, we are taught the Golden Rule: Treat others as you want them to treat you. But each situation is different, and one has to judge the level of danger and the chance that others will join in. If I'm alone with a couple of elderly people in a late night train and a gang attacks the only other young person in the carriage, what chance have I got against them? If I pull the alarm they'll turn against me too. Perhaps the most sensible thing then would be to take a photo with my mobile and go to the police with it later. That might not help the person being attacked, but it could prevent further attacks by that particular gang. At least that would seem a reasonable assumption in the circumstances.

b)

Get Involved
ANTI-SOCIAL BEHAVIOUR
CONCERNS YOU

Did you know that
▷ six out of ten Britons would not stop a teenage gang of vandals?
▷ lots of other countries have a much better record in stopping anti-social behaviour?
▷ the higher the number of people witnessing a crime the less likely people are to intervene?
▷ the youth crime rate is rising by about 10% p. a.?

We Want YOU to get involved!!

If you feel that
▷ bullying makes this school less secure than it should be
▷ vandalism makes this school less attractive than it could be
▷ you should stop unsocial behaviour.
▷ If you want to change what has to be changed
▷ if you want to make a start
▷ why don't you become a member of **YFSC** (**Y**outh **F**or **S**ocial **C**ommitment)?

For all of you who want to start to make a difference **YFSC** is organizing our school's
Get-Involved Week (June 5-9)

There will be
▷ afternoon workshops on how to deal with anti-social behaviour, with opportunities for practical experience in all aspects concerning the fight against anti-social behaviour
▷ feature films and documentaries on Thursday
▷ a **Don't Be a Bystander** disco on Friday night (free if you have attended two workshops)
Isn't that motivation enough to start working for change and get involved?

So Don't Be a Bystander - Get Involved
Get-Involved Week, at this school, June 5-9

Für die Punkte zählen folgende Aspekte:
headline
attracting attention (facts)
appealing to emotions (values)
information about "Get-Involved Week"
appeal to join group activities

Bibliographisches Institut GmbH, Dudenstraße 6, 68167 Mannheim
ISBN 978-3-411-87084-4